WOMEN ATTORNEYS SPEAK OUT!

How Practicing Law Is Different for Women Than for Men— (and Tips on How to Handle The Biggest Frustrations)

by

Judi Craig, Ph.D., MCC

Thomson West, a Thomson business, has created this publication to provide you with accurate and authoritative information concerning the subject matter covered. However, this publication was not necessarily prepared by persons licensed to practice law in a particular jurisdiction. Legalworks is not engaged in rendering legal or other professional advice, and this publication is not a substitute for the advice of an attorney. If you require legal or other expert advice, you should seek the services of a competent attorney or other professional.

ISBN 978-0-314-98737-2

ABOUT THE AUTHOR

Judi Craig, Ph.D., MCC is a Certified Senior Practice Advisor with Atticus, Inc. and a Master Certified Coach, the highest distinction available in the coaching profession. She has coached attorneys since 1996 and has a great deal of experience in advising them on how to increase their incomes, decrease their stress and time in the office, solve their staffing headaches, and take control of their practices.

Dr. Craig is the author of four nationally published books, a former syndicated columnist, and has been interviewed on over 100 radio stations. She has been a guest on *Larry King Live, The Today Show, NBC News, CBS News* and more. She is also a dynamic national keynote speaker and law firm retreat facilitator. She has been most recently published in *Texas Lawyer* and *The Connecticut Law Tribune* and writes the "Practice Boosters" practice management column in *The Complete Lawyer*.

Prior to being recruited by Atticus, Inc. for her experience with the legal community, Dr. Craig was President of The Practice Advisor, LLC, where she coached attorneys on all aspects of law practice management. She enjoys helping attorneys re-engineer their practices and speaks from experience, having built two successful professional service firms herself.

Dr. Craig received her Bachelor of Arts degree from Southern Methodist University (Phi Beta Kappa) and her Master's and Doctorate Degrees in Clinical Psychology from the University of Wisconsin. She is a graduate both of CoachU and Corporate Coach U, and served on the Corporate Coach U faculty for ten years. She is also a Master Practitioner in Neurolinguistic Programming.

Visit Dr. Craig's website at www.judicraig.com for more information.

TABLE OF CONTENTS

INTRODUCTION

What it is like to be a female attorney in today's world, particularly in comparison to being a male attorney? How are women lawyers treated—by clients, male attorneys, other women attorneys, and judges? Are their original expectations about becoming a lawyer being met, or frustrated? How are they dealing with the increasing hostility toward attorneys? What are they doing to keep a balance between the demands of their careers, their personal needs and their family commitments? What advice would they give other women who are entering, or considering, the law profession?

To find the answers to these questions, the author interviewed fifty women attorneys who work in a variety of practice areas. About eighty percent responded to an email sent to women attorneys who had attended an Atticus seminar within the past eight years (Atticus is a twenty-year-old premier education, training, and coaching company that works exclusively with attorneys) asking them to email the author if they were interested in being interviewed for the book. In order to broaden the geographic area represented by the interviewees, other potential participants were located on Martindale-Hubbell; they were called directly by the author to see if they were willing to contribute.

Eighty-two percent of the interviewees work in small firms (defined as two to ten attorneys), seven percent in medium sized firms (defined as firms with eleven to seventy-five attorneys), three percent in large firms (defined as firms with over seventy-five attorneys), and eight percent are solo practitioners. Geographically diverse, they live in fifteen states from the East Coast to the West Coast, from North to South. Twenty percent of the women have been in practice less than eleven years, forty percent have practiced for eleven to twenty years, thirty-six percent have practiced twenty-one to forty years, and four percent have practiced for over forty years. Forty-seven of the fifty interviewees were unknown to the author prior to being interviewed.

In the following pages, you will hear (mostly in their own words) how these fifty women perceive the present state of legal practice for female attorneys. They will also share their advice to other women considering (or currently practicing) law as a career.

In the process of conducting these interviews, an interesting thing happened. The interviews clearly revealed that the women's biggest frustration is how to balance their careers with their responsibilities at home. For that reason, each interviewee was asked to give their favorite "work-life balance" tip—and the author (being a Practice Management Coach for attorneys) decided to write a final chapter that would give a variety of solutions she has found helpful in working with clients (male and female) on work-life balance issues.

Remember, these are the women's *perceptions*—and we all know that perception is reality!

THE INTERVIEWEES

Deborah Ackerman	Dallas, TX	General Counsel for Southwest Airlines
Sammie Arnold	Mt. Pleasant, SC	Civil Litigation
Valerie L. Bailey-Rihn	Madison, WI	Commercial Litigation & Business Law
Theresa Baker	Ocala, FL	Trusts, Estates & Guardianship
Pam Bassel	Ft. Worth, TX	Bankruptcy Law
Odette Bendeck	West Palm Beach, FL	Family Law
Nora Bergman	St. Petersburg, FL	Employment Discrimination, Civil Rights
Susan Bernhardt	Denver, CO	Commercial Litigation
Kris Bird	San Antonio, TX	Employment Litigation

Caroline Black	Tampa, FL	Family Law
Rebecca Blair	Nashville, TN	Personal Injury & Civil Litigation
Cami Boyd	Dallas, TX	Intellectual Property & Intellectual Property Litigation
Janet Brewer	Palo Alto, CA	Estate Planning & Probate
Pamela Campbell	St. Petersburg, FL	Health Law, Probate & Guardianship
Barbara Cane	Nyack, NY	Estate Planning
Shannon Carlyle	The Villages, FL	Civil Appellate Law
Ramona Chance	Gainesville, FL	Real Property Transactions
Erin Colgan	Staten Island, NY	Divorce & Family Law
Julie Collins	Greenville, SC	Estate Planning
Carol Condon	Buffalo, NY	Family Law
Roxanne Conlin	Des Moines, IO	Employment Discrimination
Rene Coppick	Billings, MT	Real Estate & Commercial Law
Lisa Coppola	Buffalo, NY	Business Litigation
Julia Cornish	Canada (NS)	Family Law
Mary Alice David	Tallahassee, FL	Military, Family & Criminal Law
Joy Day	Nashville, TN	Product Liability Defense
Tamara Felton Dudley	St. Petersburg, FL	Divorce Law
Latonia Early-Hubelbank	Westbury, NY	Family Law
Beth Edler	Houston, TX	Commercial Litigation

Sally Busell Fox	Pensacola, FL	Real Estate Litigation & Development
Tina Graham	Phoenix, AZ	Health Law
Caryn Green	Orlando, FL	Family Law
Karen Haase	Lincoln, NE	Education Law
Eileen Hall	Dallas, TX	Family & Transactional Law
Sue Hall	San Antonio, TX	Family Law
Lyndsay Haller	Bloomington, ID	General Civil Law & Litigation
Nancy Harris	Tampa, FL	Marital & Family Law
Leigh Hilton	Denton, TX	Estate Planning
Theresa Horton	Greeneville, SC	Probate Law
Debra Kesler	Metairie, LA	Domestic Law
Jane Larson	Roseville, MN	Real Estate, Probate, Estate Planning & Elder Law
May Macaluso	Ft. Lauderdale, FL	Civil & Commercial Litigation
Karen Marvel	San Antonio, TX	Child Support Collection
Marie Mattox	Tallahassee, FL	Employment Litigation & Civil Rights
Franchelle Millinder	Columbus, SC	Elder Law
Erin O'Toole	St. Petersburg, FL	Medical Malpractice & Personal Injury
Judy Overholt	Rochester, NY	Estate Planning & Business Law
Helene Parker	Dallas, TX	Family Law
Marsha Rydberg	Tampa, FL	Business & Real Estate Litigation
Mercedes Wechsler	Orlando, FL	Family Law

CHAPTER 1

WHY A LAWYER?

Parents are known to react to an argumentative child by uttering a familiar phrase: "You should become a lawyer when you grow up!" Who would have thought that those words would be later cited as the *raison d'etre* for someone's career choice? But this is exactly what happened, according to some of the interviewees when asked their reasons for deciding to become a lawyer.

I LOVE TO ARGUE!

- My Dad always told me I would argue with a stop sign! In middle school I decided I wanted to become a lawyer—and it stuck!
- I had an unusual experience in Girl Scouts. I had a leader who I'd go to talk to about badges and she came from a family of lawyers. She would tell me, "You should be a lawyer because you can talk your way into anything." In the fifties, the law was not a career path for women, but this leader gave me permission to apply to law school.
- It was a naive reason—I liked to argue and I liked theater, so I thought I could be Perry Mason!
- A legal career was always in the back of my mind because anyone who likes to argue like me should get paid for it! I never had a fear of public speaking and enjoyed debate. Law school was kind of a floating thought until I got my

undergraduate degree in Canadian studies, which doesn't equip you for much. I worked a year in university administration, and then went to law school because I did well on the Law School Admission Test. Once in law school, it was love at first sight.

- I always loved to argue. And to write, investigate, manipulate things, and be in control. And I've always liked challenges.
- When I was young, my Dad encouraged me with comments like, "You're so argumentative, you should become a lawyer."
- Everybody always told me I argued so much!

Closely related to the "arguing" theme, other interviewees reported that they had a history of participating in debate.

- My husband watched me debate in college and he thought I should consider law as a career.
- I had a lot of experience in debate in high school and college. I loved speaking and liked the notion of pitting myself against someone else because I like to argue. Law is a civilized game of warfare.
- It started as a kid. At home we had all sorts of discussions around the dinner table—taking positions and advocating for them.

FAMILY TIES

One might also suspect that having one or more attorneys in the family, or even a close relationship with an attorney, could influence a child toward a career in law. Such was the case with several of the interviewees.

- My parents knew a lot of attorneys who seemed to have glamorous, well-respected professions.

- My father is a lawyer and so are three of my brothers. My grandfather and cousins are all lawyers. I just never knew I could do something else!
- I knew when I was around twelve-years-old that I wanted to be a lawyer. I think it is because my grandmother worked for attorneys and knew them as friends of the family; she thought I'd be good at it.
- I grew up around it—my Dad is an attorney. I'm currently in practice with him and always knew I would like it. Besides, you can't do much with an English degree.
- My Dad chose it for me. I wanted to be a schoolteacher and he didn't think teachers made enough money.
- My Grandmother was a big influence. She went to law school in the fifties, but she never had a chance to practice.
- A good friend's father was a litigator. I thought it was a fascinating job and an area where you could really help people.

INTELLECTUAL CHALLENGE

A career where one could use one's intellect was another influencing factor for many interviewees.

- I thought it would be an intellectually challenging profession. And I like the logical thinking and analysis that's required.
- It's the intellectual challenge. I was an English major undergrad, and after graduating was hired by a law firm and spent six months working with attorneys. I got interested in the process, and the attorneys I worked for fed that curiosity.
- When I graduated from college, women were expected to marry, put their husbands through law school, have kids and join the Junior League. I became a legal secretary and

did all that. Then I decided to go to law school for some intellectual challenge.

- I wanted to satisfy my intellectual curiosity. I wanted to do something that would have a great deal of intellectual content, but also human drama.
- A nun persuaded me to go to law school. She thought it would be a way to show my dramatic flair and use my brain.
- I wanted to do something challenging—something that would keep my interest—and do better for myself.
- I had an accounting undergraduate degree and wanted more challenge, so I decided to go into tax law.

THE LAW AND POLITICS

For some, it was a fascination with law and politics that sparked their interest in a legal career.

- I had an early fascination—in the seventh grade—with the Constitution. We are a nation of laws and have a legal system that can level the playing field.
- Ever since I was fourteen-years-old, I was interested in political things. So law school seemed like a natural fit.
- My ninth grade Civics teacher was really into law and politics. I was going to be a vet up to that point, and she convinced me that law is where it's at.
- I took First Amendment Law as an undergraduate and became fascinated with it. Prior to that I had worked as a musician and wanted to get out of that career. For the first six weeks of law school I wanted to quit every day—but then I got into it.

ECONOMIC CONSIDERATIONS

A desire to improve their options economically was another motivating factor for becoming an attorney. With some interviewees, "first careers" were disappointing in terms of salaries and lifestyles.

- I wanted some higher learning, and decided that a JD was more marketable than an MBA.
- I was teaching special education and liked working with kids–but there was no future in it, no advancement. My uncle is an attorney and he talked to me about law. It sounded like law would give me more options.
- I had been an elementary school teacher for three years. Being a nurse or a teacher were the options for girls when I was growing up. I became a lawyer because a woman said, "Oh, she's *just* a teacher." I did it for money and respect.
- It was a mixture of "good business opportunity" and a way to help people. And a lot better pay than being a teacher, which is what women were expected to do at the time.
- Part of me did it just because I didn't want people to think I was stupid. But I did it primarily because of the expected salary.
- I wanted to be financially independent and have a nice lifestyle.
- I wanted to improve my satisfaction—you know, the cost/benefit analysis. It angered me that I was doing my boss's job and he got the pay and all the recognition.

RESPECT AND CREDIBILITY

Other interviewees wanted a career that commands respect and credibility.

- After college I had a job as a TV news reporter, and my boss was a jackass. I remember thinking, "I'm smarter than this guy!" I wanted a job where I'm in charge of myself, and can be independent and respected.
- I am a problem solver. I thought law would be a respected, lucrative, and interesting way to problem solve professionally.
- I did it for credibility. I was working in the House of Representatives and saw that the Chair of various committees would always say, "Go ask _______ because he's a lawyer." I figured, if that's what it takes, then I'll go to law school.

THE DESIRE TO SERVE

Not unexpectedly, a strong altruistic desire for justice and for helping other people was a high priority for many of the interviewees.

- I was always an overachiever, and coming from Viet Nam, I felt it was important to make a name for myself.
- My goal was to help people. If I can help someone, I thrive—it excites me. I need to be needed.
- I thought being a lawyer was a way I could change things. In 1970, my parents moved to an unintegrated area in Long Island—and I'm Black. Our house was vandalized. I was three-years-old and it stayed with me.
- I felt law was a great profession for me so I could help people.
- I liked the idea that as a lawyer I could help others attain fairness and equity in their lives. I knew people who encouraged me to investigate this profession. Besides, I can't stand the sight of blood, so I couldn't be a doctor or a nurse.

- I just thought there was a need. My mother was a social worker, and I decided I wanted to represent victims of violence and crime. I worked for the District Attorney after law school and gained experience with domestic violence and special victims. There was a real need to represent these women in the family court arena.
- I like helping people with their problems and exercising the analytical skills you have to use as a lawyer.

UNIQUE REASONS

Finally, a number of interviewees had very specific reasons for choosing the law profession that didn't easily fall into any of the above categories.

- Because I was a good writer, my English professor, who had a son in law school, told me to go to law school because I could use my writing talent. Also, she had son in law school.
- While teaching at the college level, my students would bring me their disputes or court orders to interpret. I enjoyed helping those kids and took the LSAT on a whim. I ended up with a scholarship.
- I didn't know I wanted to be a lawyer until after I got out of law school. I went to law school not knowing what I wanted, but thought a law degree would enable me many options.
- I had a math background, but couldn't decide on a college major. Fortunately, the college let me have three majors: math, psychology, and sociology. This triple major equipped me for nothing, so I got my Masters in Social Work. One of my professors was a young, energetic guy who taught family law for the social work students. On the third day of class, I had an epiphany: I could combine

the logic of math with the more touchy-feely stuff of social work by becoming a family law attorney!

- I can't stand the sight of blood, so I couldn't be a doctor or a nurse.
- As a little girl I enjoyed reading—and you have to read a lot as a lawyer.
- I became an English teacher and decided that "I can't spend the rest of my life forcing stuff down undesiring throats!" The Employment Commission suggested I should be a secretary, but fortunately, I had a cousin in law school and decided to try that instead.
- In fourth grade, I remember having dinner with my father at a Chinese restaurant. He asked, "Now what are you going to do with your career?" and I said, "I'm going to be a corporate attorney." Maybe he was playing tapes in my ears when I was sleeping because I never wavered. And I love it.
- It was something I always wanted to do. I got my engineering degree and practiced for ten years. A good friend's death compelled me to get off my ass and do what I really wanted! I always thought law was better suited to my personality.
- I fell into law when I decided I didn't want to be a journalist. A lot of my female peers were applying to law school and encouraged me to apply, so I did.
- My first career was as a lobbyist, and I decided that to be a better one, I needed to go to law school and be a lawyer lobbyist.
- Law is my second career. I was fired for having a baby. I decided I would never be that vulnerable again, and that learning law would be the best way to protect myself.

- My ex-husband decided to get a Ph.D., and I decided I'd look like a bimbo next to women working on Ph.D.s, so I decided to go on to grad school. When I decided to be a lawyer, I was doing research and clerking in a large firm. I had a genuinely physical feeling pour over me—like being in the "zone." A light went on—it told me, "You can do this and be really good at it!"

FINAL THOUGHTS

From these women's stories, it is clear that their mutual decisions to become lawyers were motivated by a desire for work that brings intellectual challenges as well as the opportunity for the economic advantages. In addition, they wanted work that allows them to make a positive difference in the lives of the clients they serve. The latter reason should come as no surprise, given that many of our country's Founding Fathers were lawyers—and that today, lawyers are often found on Boards of Directors of both for-profit and non-profit organizations and in other positions of influence in our communities. The law is a profession where one can truly "make a difference."

CHAPTER 2

EXPECTATIONS—FRUSTRATED OR FULFILLED?

Knowing the reasons behind women attorneys' decisions to become lawyers, the next logical question is, "How is your current practice of law meeting—or not meeting—the expectations you had when you initially decided to go into law? Or the expectations you had when you graduated from law school?"

Many of the interviewees feel very positive about their practices. Others describe having to go adjust their expectations before reaching a good place. And many spoke about the hardships and stresses that come with being a lawyer—a female lawyer.

THE HIGHLY SATISFIED

Those women who find their practices extremely satisfying focus their reasons around a few themes. One is the notion of being challenged and having a diversity of experiences.

- Yes, my practice meets my expectations. I work in managing health benefits, and it is an area that is always changing. It's complicated and I always love a new twist.
- I always enjoyed school and was a bookworm. I wanted to do something that had responsibility, was important, and where I'd never be bored. All those things have come true. I joined this firm in March and feel I've finally come home; I feel fulfilled and happy.

For some, there is the internal reward that comes from forming relationships and helping people solve their problems.

- My practice in complex family law is better than I expected. It's about satisfying people—and the tremendous impact my problem solving and work has on my clients and their families. It's a great feeling to be able to do this.
- It's more than I ever could have asked for. Every day, I look forward to going to work. The variety, my practice area, and seeing the results of helping people—the internal rewards are terrific.
- My practice has provided a framework for friendships and long-lasting relationships.

Then there's the matter of economic reward.

- It more than meets my original expectations. I found out that I could do what I thought I could do, and do it pretty well. Economically, my practice is very rewarding. There's no question that the practice has exceeded every expectation regarding income.
- It's helped me to do all the things I wanted—live well, travel, be challenged, argue and investigate, be in control of things, and help others solve problems.
- I had no expectations except to make a good living and be independent—and my practice allows me to do both of those things.

Two of the participants share interesting reasons for finding their practices wholeheartedly fulfilling. For one, it's that "learning the law and practicing it as a female is very empowering." For another, it's the fact that she's been able to create an enviable work/life balance by practicing law with her husband. "My law practice is exceeding every expectation I ever had. I met my husband in law school and he recently joined our firm, so we have a great balance between work and our personal lives.

The type of practice we have enables us to have a user-friendly practice. We can wear anything we want, work any time that we choose, and set our own deadlines. We can keep our schedule flexible and we make our practice fit around our lives."

SOME CHANGE REQUIRED!

For many interviewees, a change from their original expectations had to be made in order for them to find their current practices rewarding. Their original ideas about what kind of law they wanted to practice changed after getting out in the "real world."

- My practice is better than what I expected. I never contemplated going in-house because I thought being in a firm was the way to go. But I found out that being in a large firm is very difficult if you have a family. Going in-house was a great decision because I work in a great place with cutting edge projects and the best people.
- Out of law school, I worked for the District Attorney's office and knew it wasn't what I would ultimately do. I clerked for a defense employment lawyer and really enjoyed it. I got my trial experience at the DA's office, but I am now a defense employment lawyer, which is exactly what I wanted to do.
- I didn't know what I wanted to do after law school and was open to various areas of law. I met an attorney and stumbled into Personal Injury and am very happy in my practice.
- I'm doing nothing I would have envisioned when I got out of law school. I went from big company corporate law to a solo practice.
- I didn't have any sense I'd be doing what I'm doing. I thought I'd do criminal law or help low income people get divorces. Now I represent people at the high end of

the economic scale. It is more money than I ever thought I'd make.

- I initially expected to be in court doing litigation; I didn't want an office practice. But I was micromanaged a lot by a supervising attorney and hated it. Now I'm on my own—and being in this kind of practice meets my expectations.
- I initially thought I'd do children's justice or rights work, but I got into a commercial firm and they put me in real estate closings. I decided, "No, that's where they put all the women." I fought to go into litigation and found it very intellectually interesting and challenging, but, of course, they would give the actual courtroom work to a man. It took a while before I was sent to court. When I was pregnant, they definitely didn't think I could go to court—but I did!
- My practice meets my expectations now. At first, I went with a defense firm and was very unhappy. Then I had a public practice as a U.S. attorney. Finally, I found a place in plaintiff's work and now I do nothing but trial work.
- I originally planned on litigating and joined a firm as a litigation associate. Now, I have long-term relationships with clients, and a client base made up of very nice people. It's not like litigation where you go away after the trial is over.
- I enjoyed the intellectual aspects of law but didn't like the day-to-day practice of law. My area of practice was too acrimonious and I knew I would be arguing all day, whether I was in court or not. So I got certified as a mediator and teach as an adjunct professor.
- My practice is great now, but it was a long, tortuous path to get here. I clerked for a judge, which was wonderful, and then worked in a big firm, which was intellectually

exciting but very difficult and hostile to a mother with young children. In the early eighties there were no women attorneys in the firm who had young children; all the male attorneys had wives who were home taking care of everything. Working in a corporate setting didn't speak to my goals of wanting to help individuals. I wanted an environment that was creative and nurturing, and mostly non-combative. So I decided to set up my own practice where I can create it the way I wanted it to be, from the stationery to the ethical values. I work out of my home, but have a private entrance to my office, making it a very professional environment. My clients deal with a lot of emotional stuff, and I set up my office like a living room. The setting puts people at ease and they tell me their hopes, dreams, and fears.

- I've changed a lot. I worked in children's law while in law school, but I found out pretty quickly that it was something I enjoyed doing as a volunteer, but not as a career. I continue to do volunteer work as a guardian *at litum*, but my career is now litigating.

One interviewee reveals that her ideas about a law practice changed after she had a family. "I'm now very sure that in any decision I make, my family comes first and my career comes second."

Another participant shares that "for your practice to be fulfilling, you have to find a way to make it happen. My state is not that progressive in terms of law concepts—we have an old guard with a vested interest in seeing things stay the same. We don't even have no-fault divorce. It's like pulling teeth to change the system."

IT'S JUST HARD!

Interestingly, over thirty percent of the interviewees comment on how hard it is to practice law, and its requisite level of stress. For some, it's the *business* aspect *of* law that they've found difficult.

- Practicing law still meets the intellectual challenges I was expecting. But it is unrealistic to go into the law thinking that you're going to contribute to the overall good all the time. A law practice is a business and you have to look at it as one.
- Practicing law is about 180 degrees different than what I expected! I didn't anticipate the business aspect. I thought it would be a matter of helping clients, but there's so much more to it—like other attorneys, paralegals, secretaries, office management. I just wasn't prepared for all that.
- It's so much more difficult than I had thought due to the demands on my time. Plus I had no appreciation for the business aspects.
- Running a business is definitely not in the starry-eyed view of the new law graduate.

Others participants point out the naiveté of their original ideas of what made up a law practice.

- I was very naive. Much of a law practice is very unlike Perry Mason. A litigation practice is much about writing and analysis and very little about courtroom tactics. Only a small percent of my cases ever go to trial. When I started out, I think there was more of a sense that the legal system was altruistic, working toward ideals. Then the reality set in, and today it is very discouraging. We are under so many mandates and forms, which are intended to streamline the process for clients, but have made the process more cumbersome. The idea is to have intellectual challenges, but court is really concerned with resolution and not so much with legal analysis. It's so frustrating.

- A law practice is not nearly as prestigious as I had thought. The world of law isn't what you see on television. It is much more complicated and the knowledge base is formidable. I was kind of shell-shocked.
- It's totally different than what I expected. I had a Perry Mason view of law. I thought I wanted to do family law, and am now doing something completely different. I had the feeling that law would help people, and discovered that it isn't necessarily so.

Some of the interviewees find that practicing law is difficult because of discrimination toward women attorneys—or just because of the general disrespect given to lawyers.

- Well, I don't make as much money as I probably should, but that's not my primary goal. I love to craft a business and bring people together as a team. But I wasn't expecting the level of disrespect that attorneys get.
- I didn't have a clue when I graduated. Law school was collegial, supportive, and fun. To go into a law firm environment was like a plunge into cold water! I went into a seventy-five-year-old firm that was very much a male domain; I was the second woman they'd ever hired. It was shocking. And I had no clue about business issues. I just saw the world of law as a continuation of law school, and it wasn't. The partners had never had to think of a maternity policy—until I got pregnant. I had two kids and they let me work part time, but the message was that "real lawyers don't work part-time."

- My practice has met my expectations in terms of fulfilling my potential and in terms of my own professional growth. Where it has not met my expectation is the way women are still facing a lot of adversity within the profession and the court system, which is still a male-dominated area. I'm fortunate to have found a family-friendly firm that understands the pull on professional women. But the "mommy track" is somewhat slower.

Finally, many of the interviewees are struggling with the stress of a law practice,

- Professionally, law has met my expectations, even exceeded them. But personally, it is far more taxing than I would have imagined. Going into the profession, I didn't understand how much a litigator's life gets taken over by the schedules of others and how much the case outcomes weigh on you and your other family members.
- I fell into family law and loved the practice—but what I don't love is the high stress. It's difficult to meet client expectations, remain ethical, and do the right thing. So I often don't meet my clients' expectations. My practice meets my expectations as a lawyer, but do I need this stress? Absolutely not.
- Financially it meets my expectations and I don't have to work eighty hours a week to make a livable income. But the stress is much more than I expected. Even if you're hired part-time, you really work full-time and just get paid less.
- I have the respect and status I expected. But I feel so swamped with my roles as a mother, a lawyer, and a businessperson. Plus I'm in the Reserves.
- I had more intellectual challenge and enjoyed research while in law school. Today there's not much time for

thoughtful analysis and creativity because there are so many things pulling for my attention.

- Practicing law is very different from what I expected. It is a lot more demanding. My perception was that law would be along the lines of a regular business—but it's a lot more hours than nine to five.

A FINAL THOUGHT

Many of the interviewees found that practicing law was quite different from what they had originally anticipated as law students—and clearly, some were still struggling with some areas of their practices. Yet, the fact is that none of them want to quit. In spite of their trials and tribulations, they all plan to hang in there and continue their practices.

CHAPTER 3

THE ADVANTAGES OF BEING FEMALE!

"What advantages, if any, do you think there are to being a female attorney as opposed to a male attorney?" The vast majority (about ninety-five percent) of the interviewees think that being a woman lawyer has definite advantages. They perceive that male attorneys often inadvertently give them the advantage by simply underestimating how effective women attorneys can be! They also agree that females have distinct gifts and skills that can be an asset when serving their clients. In addition, they believe women attorneys often have a specific client selection advantage—that is, that clients will specifically choose a female attorney either because they expect women to be more sensitive and compassionate, and/or because they believe that there are specific advantages to having a woman represent their interests.

THE POWER OF BEING UNDERESTIMATED

- Many men underestimate us, and then we have the element of surprise.
- As a woman, it is sometimes a real advantage not to be taken that seriously. I look like a sweet little old lady, and not much of a threat.
- If people have lower expectations for women, then your accomplishments can look more noteworthy. A male opposing counsel who hasn't worked with you previously may be especially likely to underestimate you.

- I've sometimes found that opposing counsel will underestimate you, which I just laugh at and use to my advantage.
- Some older men think I'm young, female and harmless, so they're off guard. They'll ask questions and say things they'd never say to a man.
- Older men who are used to fighting with other men often don't know how to take us women. They really underestimate us.
- I'm often underestimated—especially since I'm a Southern woman—and it's quite an advantage!
- Being female puts me in a position of advantage in court where a lot of male attorneys have very low expectations of me. I feel less pressure to have to impress them with my abilities.
- My adversaries often underestimate me, and that's an enormous advantage. I'm smarter than some and can pull the proverbial rabbit out of a hat!

Most of the interviewees think that being female brings with it certain unique abilities that help them become better lawyers, and that set them apart from the majority of men. Specifically, they mention that women are more likely to value their intuition, to empathize and nurture, to be relationship-oriented, and to get their clients to "open up." Some believe that women have unique problem-solving and communication skills distinct from those used by the majority of men.

TUNING IN TO INTUITION

- Women have certain gifts that are very valuable, such as intuition and the ability to read people better in nonverbal settings.
- We have emotional intuition and a sensitivity that can be used in negotiation and to build a client's understanding.

It's huge. Instead of the linear thinking of one plus one equals two, using an intuitive strategy can often be more successful. And I think women are more flexible and facile with their styles of communication.

EMPATHIZING AND NURTURING

- I think women can be more empathetic towards clients in dealing with personal as well as legal issues. For example, I went to someone's bedside in ICU; as a woman and a mother, I was able to help in a different way. Women can sometimes go the extra mile on a personal level where a man would not.
- In family law, the advantage is that I can empathize with my client in ways males probably can't or aren't willing to. It's an attitude thing—and I can empathize more with what life will look like as a single parent after a divorce.
- When there's a crisis, people want the Mom or the emotional nurturer.
- My perspective is that I have the ability to nurture relationships in the type of work I do (estate planning) and that is not seen as a weakness in my area. And I don't have to be constantly arguing or overly aggressive, which would surely be perceived as a negative. It is a natural fit for my personality.
- Women attorneys tend to bond better with their clients. They can usually do a better job of putting people at ease because they are more empathetic.
- Women get more license to be nurturing and supportive—even able to hug somebody or put an arm around them. It comes naturally for women.

- Emotions are expected in family law. Many men would be very reluctant to show sadness or distress, or to cry in front of another man. The ability to nurture is a definite advantage that allows women to be perceived as less threatening.
- Many clients tend to look for empathy; they feel that women will understand better.
- Women are generally more perceptive to and have greater insight into their clients' needs. And women tend to be a little more caring. Men are more easily able to make it strictly business; when they leave at the end of the day, many of them couldn't care less about the client.

BUILDING RELATIONSHIPS

- Women are more adept at seeing the patterns of relationships in conflict-oriented situations. Because of their intuitive and compassionate natures, solutions to people problems may come more easily to women, as may figuring out how to sell solutions to a client.
- Women have the luxury of creating long-term relationships and many men don't.
- Women are just naturally better at relationship-building and connecting with people.

GETTING OTHERS TO "OPEN UP"

- Clients feel more comfortable telling me the very personal details of their lives. I don't see them doing that with male lawyers.
- In my estate practice, it is easier for people to let down their guards and talk to me. I've had many male business-executive-clients who will close the door and express their vulnerabilities, which they may never be able

to express to another man. With female clients, there's a "just us girls" feel.

- I am able to put a witness at ease when a male lawyer cannot. When there are highly charged emotions, I can get people to open up.
- Many clients are just more willing to confide in a female.
- Since I'm blonde, I just act dumb when doing depositions, and people will tell me more information than their attorneys want them to.

PROBLEM SOLVING AND COMMUNICATING

- Women are just more adept at building consensus and making things work.
- It is easier for women to find places of compromise when resolving disputes. It's not foreign for women to talk about issues in order to resolve them.
- Women attorneys see the bigger picture more clearly than men who might be hung up on some detail. Women tend to see both sides of a position sooner.
- I diffuse situations and close matters successfully, while many men don't create the necessary rapport.
- Women have the ability to make people behave more sociably toward one another, which is great in settlement situations. Women are more inclined to chat, which draws people together. Men don't chat.
- The perception is that women will be more responsive, better listeners, and more sensitive.
- Men and women look at things differently. Problems sometimes have more than one solution, and a woman will see a different approach. Women are also multi-taskers who are comfortable doing a couple of things at the same time.

- The advantage for women is their problem-solving skill set. Men seem to be trained to have that adversarial mentality. Men are looking at how to win, while women are looking at how to solve the issue.
- Women think differently than men. We have some sensitivities and analytic abilities that work for our clients.
- In litigation, women tend to be more "Let's get this resolved for our client!" and less concerned about their own egos. With men, the chest-thumping gets into play.
- I think we women have a more realistic perspective on issues and cases.
- I am more open to creative business solutions for my clients than many male litigators.
- Women can be subtly persuasive and manipulative; a good woman lawyer will use that to her advantage.
- A lot of times, women will look for more practical solutions. They don't need to posture as much as men do. They do a better job for their clients than do men who think, "I need a victory to show the opposing counsel who's boss!"

CLIENT SELECTION FACTORS

Three of the fifty women interviewed think that clients do not have a different set of expectations regarding female versus male attorneys. All three gave the same reason for this belief—that client selection has more to do with the length of time an attorney is in practice rather than an attorney's gender.

However, the other forty-seven interviewees believe that clients often specifically select women attorneys over male attorneys for one of two reasons. First, many clients believe a female lawyer will show more compassion and sensitivity than her male counterpart.

- Clients expect women attorneys to be more compassionate. They think they can spill their guts and the woman attorney will bleed with them. They don't spill their guts as easily to a man—and if they do, the man will surely not be bleeding with them.
- They probably expect women to be gentler than and not as blunt as a man would be.
- People expect more sympathy from a woman. They want you to identify with their emotions, and are sometimes surprised when a woman is pragmatic and tries to draw them away from emotionality. Sometimes women only want to work with a female attorney because they are too bruised by the men in their lives and don't want to be hurt again.
- They expect more handholding, more empathy.
- Clients expect a little more nurturing. Many women are more comfortable telling a woman private matters.
- Women clients think a woman will empathize with their situation more. I do have women come in who want to make sure I'm a bulldog. Women want somebody aggressive, but are also concerned about the empathy factor.
- They expect me to feel their pain and hold their hand—but my reputation is that I'm a bulldog. I do try to make them feel better afterwards.
- I have older women clients, and they expect me to be more sensitive to them than a male would be.
- They expect women attorneys to be more sensitive and less aggressive. With women clients, there's an expectation of being cozy or girlfriend-like. You don't have the problem with flirtatiousness that men have with women clients.
- I think it matters in family law but not business law. People expect women to show more sympathy. Some

women want male attorneys because they're looking for protectors.

- Clients expect more emotion and sympathy from a female lawyer.
- Some male clients hire a woman attorney because they're looking for a mother.
- Clients may think a woman will be more sympathetic to their viewpoints—but I don't think it is true.
- Clients expect women attorneys to act more like counselors or therapists.
- Clients expect a woman attorney to be their friend, not just a legal representative. That's good because it helps develop a solid relationship with trust. People won't confide in a man the same way because of a lack of that type of bonding.

The interviewees believe that some clients will select a woman attorney over a male attorney for another reason: the belief that there are some tactical advantages to hiring a woman.

- They think it is an advantage to have a female if the opposing counsel is female—but women lawyers can be really tough on one another.
- There's an expectation that I'll be more flexible in the time of day I'll meet with them—and that I will be more understanding of their personal issues that may not be directly related to their legal issues.
- Over the years, clients have told me that they hired me because I'm a woman and they knew I'd pay more attention to them and be more detailed. There is a perception that women will focus more.
- Clients think they have a better chance of settling (rather than going to court) if their attorney is a female.

- Clients also seem to expect women to service them on a more immediate basis—maybe they think our time is not as occupied. It could be that they just think we're better organized than a man.
- Clients expect a certain level of politeness and manners from a female attorney. I don't have the ability to vent and fume in a mediation as much as one of my male colleagues who rants, raves, and throws around a few foul words.
- Clients expect a woman lawyer to be a better listener than a male lawyer. Clients expect female attorneys to listen to their stories more patiently than a man.
- Clients expect a realistic, personal, and no-holds-barred type of communication from female attorneys.
- Clients expect woman attorneys to be more communicative than male attorneys.
- There's a perception in estate planning that a woman attorney will do a better job than a male attorney because women are more used to dealing with emotional family issues.
- Many clients think they'll get a better level of service from a woman lawyer—and I think they're right!

FINAL THOUGHTS

Two of the interviewees mention some especially unique advantages to being a female attorney.

- Women have a better ability to strike a balance between their personal lives and their law practices. Men tend to identify themselves more as "lawyers," while women tend to see their law practices as just one aspect of their personalities.
- In sexual discrimination or sexual harassment cases, it is an advantage to be a woman attorney. I know what I'm

> talking about from a woman's perspective. Businesses sense this and are turning more and more to female lawyers.

Finally, one interviewee who initially could not think of any advantages in being a female attorney exclaimed, "Wait! I've got one! One time I was in a trial and losing badly. But I went into labor and the case was postponed!"

CHAPTER 4

THE DOWNSIDE

Asked about the disadvantages of being a woman attorney, many of the eighty percent who had been in practice more than ten years prefaced their answers by stating that practicing law today is much improved over what it was when they started. This statement was equally true for those practicing eleven to twenty years as for those practicing twenty-one to forty years, suggesting that positive change has been taking place over the last forty years.

While almost all of the interviewees agree that there are definite advantages to being a female attorney, none of them had any problems coming up with a variety of disadvantages.

GENDER DISCRIMINATION

According to the many interviewees, gender discrimination still exists in the twenty-first century.

- In my firm there's a very real good-old-boys' club. I've been told that some clients might not feel comfortable with me because they would have to hold back their cursing. I'm often the one doing the work—but the case is presented by one of the male attorneys.
- I think there are higher expectations for women attorneys. Judges, clients, and male attorneys are less likely to cut you any slack if you miss a deadline, don't return a phone call, or speak out of line. But, "Oh, he's out

golfing today," is fine. A typical example: Both clients had to be present for a court hearing. My client had to take off from work and lose pay. Her husband, the other attorney's client, didn't show up. But the judge accepted the excuse that he must not have gotten his email!

- Male attorneys really stick up for one another—if one commits an indiscretion, another will help find him a job. Men don't do that for women—and women don't do that for one another.
- Some male attorneys think the women in their firms are just there to earn pin money.
- There's reluctance on the part of those sending lawyers business to send it to women. Everyone loses, but when a woman loses you often hear someone ask the client, "Why didn't you hire a male lawyer?"
- Law is still a male-dominated profession. You're expected to play the game to win, no matter what—just like in football.
- There's a culture that persists where men are seen as the litigators and the ones with trial experience, and the women are viewed as the "office attorneys." It's a big hurdle we still need to overcome.
- Women are still perceived as second chairs even when they are partners. Men have an unspoken advantage.
- Some people just respond better to male lawyers—the "boys' club" kind of thing.
- I often feel discounted when I'm in the presence of male attorneys—overlooked, not included as an equal, not a member of the "good old boys." If you want to break in, you have to participate in male activities—like football or golf. The idea of getting a group of attorneys together and going to the art museum just doesn't happen.

- If I have to make a hard decision, then I'm a "bitch"—even if it is with staff. A man doesn't have this problem.
- When I was in the corporate and big-firm environment, every day I'd hear some kind of comment that dealt with my being a woman. For example, if I were at the office late, people would say, "So who's cooking dinner?" If I left a six o'clock, they'd say, "Oh, gotta get home to the kids, huh?"
- A lot of businesses still think you have to have a male to defend you. It's hard for a woman to walk into a courtroom and have equal footing with a male attorney.
- Males won't be chastised for their comments in court even though they are just as stinging and brutal as women have made—and been chastised for.
- Some older clients are more uncomfortable with a female attorney.
- I don't think women are used to having their own authority. They're not trained in how to handle it in a way that feels comfortable—and they're not very good at delegating.
- Clients may try to bully or intimidate you. And some seem to think that male attorneys are just smarter.
- There's still a question about whether women can be successful in the courtroom, even though a lot are. If a woman is too strident, some people think she is unattractive—so you have to walk a fine line.
- Women sometimes have to temper their positions for fear of looking unreasonable, whiney, or "bitchy." We tend to want to compromise, rather than face off at a hearing in front of a judge.

- Women who are assertive are perceived as being aggressive and difficult.
- Women in law firms are not given plum assignments because men assume that the women don't want to travel or work long hours, especially if the women have children.
- There is initial prejudice against a woman attorney just because she's female.

THE CREDIBILITY ISSUE

Other interviewees mention that credibility is still an issue for them.

- Women just aren't taken as seriously. Period.
- Though better than twenty years ago, men still benefit from an inherent credibility, while women have to work harder to gain the trust of jurors and judges.
- I've found that I have to work harder to make people respect me as much as they respect a male attorney.
- I don't like it if I'm not taken seriously. What I've discovered is that men will attempt to bluff their way and think that you're not smart enough to figure it out.
- I get so frustrated in meetings when I say something and have it ignored—but when a man says the same thing, it's brilliant!
- We're not always taken seriously, though it is not as much of a problem when you're an old broad. I now wear pink just as much as I want. If they underestimate me, it's an advantage because they don't see me coming!
- When you go into a deposition or a courtroom with a bunch of men, you have to be one step ahead of them because there is still the impression that you are of lesser quality than they are.

- For the general public, you have to work a little harder establishing relationships to ensure that they come back to you instead of a male lawyer.
- With male attorneys you haven't worked with before, they test you—and not very subtly. With men you often have to prove yourself very quickly or they'll try to bully you. They want to test how aggressive you can be in advocating for your client. I've had judges stop the bullying from opposing counsel and say, "Not with this one, Counsel!"
- Older male attorneys don't take women seriously. They still think you're the court reporter or secretary.
- There's no question that when some of my clients don't like my answer, they go check it out with a male attorney they know. One told me I was "too ethical"; I wonder if he would have said that to a man. There's a tendency to think that a woman won't go as far as she should.
- Sometimes you have to work harder to have the same respect and advantages that men get just because they're males.
- Lack of respect. Nobody ever confuses a court reporter with a male attorney!

THE FLIP SIDE OF EMPATHY

Ironically, while the women feel they bring their emotional sensitivity and sense of caring to the practice of law as definite strengths, there can be a flip side.

- We tend to internalize more than men, especially in litigation. You can't win one hundred percent of the time, and women get closer to their clients. So it is harder when we lose.

- Women are more emotional and we really have to put a check on ourselves so that we use it to our advantage. I need to ask myself, "Why am I feeling that?" because if I can't harness the emotion, it can be a disadvantage. We have to be careful not to lose our perspectives.
- I think women are better at negotiating and compromising, but sometimes it is really better to be more positional.
- Clients have an expectation that a woman lawyer will do some things for free or for less money than their male colleagues. They think, "If you really care, you won't charge me so much!"
- Women have to struggle with how to be adversarial without being aggressive and personalizing the conflict. It's harder for women to leave it at the door and go have a beer afterward.
- The flip side of being empathetic is that you can get so into feeling sorry for your client that you don't do a good job—you enable them to be victims and stay victims, instead of getting on with their lives.

THE SOCIAL SCENE

Several of the interviewees mentioned that there are social disadvantages to being a female lawyer.

- In a social setting (as opposed to a business networking event), a natural conversation about what you do for a living doesn't occur. As part of my marketing, I once spent $1,000 on a ticket to a social event specifically to meet some movers and shakers but nobody asked me what I do. I only got questions about what I thought of the décor and the food! Unless you have someone to introduce you as, "This is ___________, an attorney," there isn't a good way to let people know that you're a lawyer. Men are always asked what they do for a living!

- Some males are quick to accuse you of sleeping with your clients.
- Some male attorneys don't want to travel with you—maybe they just have jealous spouses.
- Well, I can't go to the restroom or play golf with the guys! That's a disadvantage!

APPEARANCE COUNTS

Different standard for females than for males in regard to physical appearance can be another disadvantage.

- I hear stories that there are judges who still require women attorneys to wear a skirt in the courtroom. Some of my friends say they'll never wear slacks because they're just not sure what the judge will think.
- I'm 4 feet 11 inches and weigh 100 pounds. Sometimes I wonder if male clients perceive me as weaker.
- For young women starting out, there are some land mines you have to be careful of—especially if you are physically attractive.
- I have long hair and like to wear high heels, and a dear male friend said, "I couldn't go to trial with you because you are pretty and a jury won't like you." So as a woman, you have to be very self-conscious about what you wear.

WOMEN HAVE TO "DO IT ALL"

Some interviewees mention a clear disadvantage for women attorneys simply because of the increased roles and demands that women take on in addition to their work obligations.

- Most women have more responsibilities than do men. Most women I went to law school with either don't practice or they've gone with a corporate or government position so that they don't have so many demands on their time.

- Having to do two jobs—the kids are the second job! There are two competing interests and it's not that way for male attorneys.
- I know very few women in my law school class who are still practicing because of the extreme time demands of being a lawyer. It's difficult unless you have a maid at home or no kids. I see women being crushed by the load they're trying to carry.
- There's a realistic disadvantage in that some women just simply try to take on too much!

THE "B" WORD!

For several decades, communication experts have talked about the fact that assertive women are perceived as aggressive. There is a difference.

Consider the following restaurant scenario: You order a steak medium well. When it arrives, it is rare. An aggressive response would be for you to call the waiter and loudly say, "Do you call this bleeding thing on my plate medium well? What's the matter with your cook? Can't you people get anything right?"

An assertive response might be to call the waiter to the table and calmly state, "I ordered my steak medium well and it is quite rare. Would you please ask the chef to cook it some more?"

For women, the problem is that even the assertive response may be perceived as aggressive. The stereotype is that a female is to be acquiescent and, if she does ask for something different, to be apologetic about asking.

Now consider the position of a woman attorney. Her job is adversarial by nature. While women in any profession may be seen as "too aggressive" when they assert themselves, this issue becomes maximized for the woman attorney who is advocating for her client.

In 2003, NBA basketball star Kobe Bryant was accused of rape. The media dubbed his defense attorney, a woman, a "pit bull with pearls." The male District Attorney was not given any derogatory labels. For a man, being argumentative, assertive, and bold are seen as strengths. For a woman, these same skills lead to unflattering labels like "bitch" and, yes, "pit bull with pearls."

Here's how the interviewees put it.

- Some stereotypes you have to worry about; if I'm assertive, I'm seen as a "bitch."
- A decent amount of sexism is still around. For example, if a woman takes a position and sticks with it during a case—in other words, takes an aggressive approach as a man would—she'll be seen as a "bitch." Women can be equally effective as men, but they have to be more conscious of how they're doing their jobs and how they are perceived. If I'm in a negotiation, mediation, or in front of jury, I want the decision to be in my client's favor and can't have them thinking I'm a "bitch." This whole thing greatly affects how we practice on a day-to-day basis.
- Some clients expect women in litigation to be kind of hard-core and more mannish and "bitchy," that is, we have to look and walk tough. I just don't fit that profile.
- When a woman is the lawyer and takes a strong position, she's a "bitch." When a man acts the same way, he's "strong."
- If we're too aggressive, we're perceived as being a "bitch." But if we're not aggressive, we're perceived as "weak." You just can't win!
- There's the "bitch" factor—so many clients think women are catty and emotional rather than professional and objective. And when they hire a woman, these clients

want you to be as angry as they are because they expect you to be emotional. They don't expect that from a man because they perceive men as less emotional to begin with.

- Women can't be aggressive without losing credibility and being called "bitchy." But if we are not aggressive, we lose some ground in an exchange or a negotiation. It's a fine line we women have to all walk.
- We still have to be careful in the way we present ourselves—not as shrill and "bitchy." Women lawyers are more accepted now. But I've seen some women, in their aggressiveness, come off in ways that I think are inappropriate and ineffective.
- It's simple: If we're assertive, we come across as "bitchy."
- There's still a tendency, especially in rural areas, that a woman will be a sweet little lady who will not be able to go toe-to-toe with opposing counsel. Law is still a male-dominated profession and people have trouble dealing with you if you're not behaving according to your gender role. A woman has to use her gender effectively and not try to be a man, or men will think of her as a "bitch."
- Despite what everyone puts out as propaganda, there is a double standard when men and women walk into the courtroom. Women are not on equal footing, at least initially. A man can stand there and be aggressive and assertive, but if a woman does it, then she's a "bitch."

From these comments, it is clear that even in the twenty-first century, women attorneys still risk being called "bitches" just for doing their jobs!

CLIENT SELECTION FACTORS

Although the interviewees agree that many clients seek them out specifically because they are female, they also know that some clients still prefer male attorneys.

- Some clients don't give us the same assumption of ability that they give to a male attorney.
- Many clients think you're not as competent as a man. You have to earn their respect and stand your ground.
- Clients sometimes expect that they can intimidate or bully a female attorney.

Many of the interviewees believe there's a concern on the part of clients that females attorneys might not be "tough enough" compared to their male counterparts.

- You'll notice that the killer litigators on television or in books are all men! You have to work to overcome the view that clients think they'd be better off with a man.
- In litigation, women aren't generally perceived as strong and don't command the respect and fear that men do.
- Some clients expect women in litigation to look mannish or bitchy, and walk tough. A profile that doesn't apply to me. Some clients have told me that they prefer me to a male attorney because they view me as a wolf in sheep's clothing.
- To compensate for the fact that they're not aggressive enough, some women look for a tough female attorney.
- Sometimes I have clients who don't think I'm tough enough—but they'd be fine with it if a man did or said the same things.
- Some clients think you have to be forceful to be effective, so they criticize a woman if they don't think she's tough enough.

- Clients want to make sure a female attorney is assertive, maybe even aggressive. You have to prove yourself if you're a female.
- If you're a female in family law, clients expect you to be one helluva Ball Buster.

A few of the interviewees think that clients hold women attorneys to a higher standard than they do male attorneys.

- They cut you less slack and call you on things. They'll complain more to a woman attorney. If they don't like a man lawyer, they'll just find another attorney rather than complain.
- Clients don't give us as much leeway as they would give a male attorney.
- Clients demand more of a female attorney because of the "mommy complex." You're expected to do a thousand different things in half the time where someone would cut some slack for a male. Clients are less forgiving about us having other demands on our schedules when they say, "Can you get this and that done?"

And then there's the matter of money. Several interviewees state that clients expect a woman's legal services to cost less than those of a male attorney.

- Clients expect to get a better bargain from a woman.
- There's a subtle expectation that I'll be less expensive than a male attorney.
- Clients expect that you'll be cheaper than a man.

Finally, two interviewees mention that women attorneys are sometimes hired to serve a not-so-hidden agenda.

- Women clients expect women attorneys to identify with them, but not necessarily for the right reasons. For example, they'll try to get complete control of their children and push the father out of the picture—"You know that mothers know best." Or they'll expect you to act punitively if their spouse has a girlfriend. Some of the most reluctant payers are women who don't have custody of their kids. And sometimes a man whose been accused of abusing his wife will hire a female lawyer so he can look better to the judge.

- Often male clients want a female lawyer because they think it makes them appear as more reasonable and sympathetic to a judge. Of course, judges just laugh at that!

THOSE LAWYER JOKES!

Making fun of attorneys seems to be the "in" thing to do these days. Whether at a cocktail party, on a coffee break, attending a business meeting or watching a stand-up comic's routine, chances are you'll hear a negative lawyer joke. The law is a profession that is maligned more than any other.

So how does all this negative press and conversation affect a woman lawyer's self image? Unfortunately, there is a strong negative effect for about twenty percent of the interviewees.

- I've told many people that I almost have to apologize for being a lawyer. I'll say something like, "I'm a lawyer, but I'm really a nice person!"
- It impacts me very negatively, unfortunately. You just find yourself apologizing for being a lawyer, not really wanting to tell people. It's even worse for a plaintiff's lawyer. I have a lot of lawyer friends who won't tell anyone, especially their doctors, that they are personal injury lawyers.
- I range from being ticked off to being appalled at the perception and feelings people have about us.
- This has been a real issue for me—a very negative impact—because of my field and also because I'm a single

woman. When I go to a mixer or cocktail party, people tell me all this negative stuff. I'll walk down the hall and someone will say, "How can you do that matrimonial stuff?" When my practice was not going well five years ago, I did not have a mentor to help me develop, and I had no specific goals. Working with my Practice Coach has helped me turn around that negative self-image. I'm learning how to market and to feel good about my practice. My Coach has given me support. She helps me be able to tap into the good parts of what I am doing and see how my practice *is* helping other people.

- It's really hard—especially if you're trying to live your ideal. You walk up to someone, tell them you're an attorney, and they'll say, "Let me tell you a joke," and it's always about greed. I was shocked at first; you wouldn't walk up to a black person and say, "Let me tell you a great black joke." Total strangers tell me jokes that slam my profession. The greed issue really bothers me.
- I no longer use the word "attorney" when introducing myself.
- I find it hurtful. I consider family law difficult because of clients' issues, and I know how much dedication it takes. You can't have a free society without lawyers! It is disheartening that a small number of bad eggs have been allowed to be representative of our profession. It is very troubling.
- Sometimes I don't feel as proud to say I'm an attorney as I should. I'm almost apologetic because of those negative perceptions.
- I feel like I'm always combating that negative stereotype when networking with non-attorneys. I have to overcome whatever the latest horrible thing some lawyer did

that's in the news. I just don't want to be affiliated with all that negativity.

Many of the women who felt negatively impacted added that they consciously attempt to make up for the negative influences they see resulting from these lawyer jokes.

- You have to be sensitive to the perception of lawyers when you are in front of people. When they tell one of those negative jokes, I've asked, "Have you had a negative experience with a lawyer?" This impacts every client.
- Sometimes I make a point to talk about how important lawyers are to building our country and communities, and that there are bad apples in all professions.
- Well, it probably affects me less than personal injury attorneys. Because of all the negative press, I have educated other people about the legal system, what attorneys do, and how we do it.
- It just makes me more determined to prove my professionalism—and on top of that, I'm blonde!
- I think I'm extra careful in informing my clients that I'm ethical. People need to know that we attorneys are held to a very high ethical standard, and I try to let people know that every day.
- I work with a Business Ethics award committee, which awards businesses that have high ethical practices. I feel I'm balancing the negative perception of lawyers by my work on that committee.
- If people say something negative to me about being a lawyer, then I point that out that we're still respected like doctors are respected.
- I find myself in social settings trying to explain, in a non-threatening way, why a preconception about attorneys

is in error. And I point out the benefits they've been afforded in life because of the work of lawyers.

- I like to point out that when people are in trouble, an attorney is the first person they call. They tell jokes until they need us.
- Clients expect me to be mean and snotty sometimes, so I go out of my way to be as patient, professional, and non-threatening as I can be.
- I try a little harder in order to overcome those negative perceptions. The honesty issue is important to me. I also shave off a lot of my cost because I'm not out there to make tons of money—I don't think God wants me to be rich. I think many female lawyers are more sensitive to the cost issues of clients, as well as their emotional pain and suffering, than are men lawyers. Women discount more and are more flexible.
- When working with lawyers who personify those bad images, I try very hard not to be perceived as they are.
- My reply is, "Yeah, just wait until you need us. Then you'll want us!"
- It is crucial that we put the honor back in our profession. I like to address issues of my practice with friends and people directly—put it right out in the open. I don't mind laughing at the jokes, but they bring up issues we need to talk about. I am passionate about being professional. Normally I will follow up a negative joke with some discussion and not just leave it there.
- If I do pro-bono work, my fee is "No lawyer jokes!"

And a few of the interviewees comment on the fact that some of the negative perceptions about lawyers are well deserved.

- I think things are even worse than what the press perceives. Over the course of the years, I've seen far more of a business orientation and a lessening of the professionalism for attorneys. It' all about how much can we make rather than what can we do for the client.

- The public thinks we make too much money and that we're mean and snotty. Other members of our profession have brought on part of our bad press—the way they treat paralegals as well as their clients.
- There are enough bad attorneys to give all of us a bad name; I deal with some of them every day. I must admit that there are those who reflect poorly on the profession.
- This issue of lawyer reputation is nationwide and the reality is that stereotypes come from truth. The sharks and pit bull lawyers are out there just like in any profession. The irony is that people will criticize and joke about lawyers—but most successful TV programs are about lawyers and many people want their own children to be lawyers! It's a real love/hate situation. You always hear the bad before you hear the good. The legal profession is concerned about the image of the profession. For every one bad situation that you hear about, hidden from the public eye are a bunch of lawyers who are doing good in the community.
- The negative publicity is well deserved. There are enough lawyers out there that do their jobs poorly. I love it when people tell me I'm so much better than what they expected from all those rumors.
- A lot of jokes are well deserved, but I think it is unfortunate for the profession.
- Well, I have met some of the lawyers who are the subject of these jokes!

The majority of women, however, did not feel personally affected by the lawyer jokes. These jokes don't bother them—and a few even enjoy them!

- Those jokes really haven't impacted my professional self-image. I'm a "rules girl," so I follow the law and my own rules of ethics and professional conduct. I have a moral compass that I use to guide myself.
- That negative stuff really doesn't affect me. I view myself as an individual even though our industry doesn't have a good reputation. I keep myself above the industry standards.
- I look at it this way: There's good and bad in every profession.
- There are good and bad people in every career. I find those jokes just as funny as the non-attorneys do.
- I'm able to shrug it off, unless I hear a lot of it in a short period of time.
- I collect those lawyer jokes and we put them on the bulletin board in our workroom. I figure we lawyers are the only group that people can pick on anymore—you can't tell ethnic jokes and be politically correct.
- The only thing that bothers me is when clients think I overcharge.
- Most of those negative jokes have to do with litigators, and I'm not a litigator.
- Clients send me lawyer jokes, and I'm not offended.
- I am blessed in what I do with very good relations with my clients. I often get a hug as well as my check. In a litigious society, you can't blame everything on lawyers. Behind those lawyers are clients who want revenge and more.
- It's a shame, and the Bar should do more to try to alleviate those negative perceptions about lawyers. But it doesn't affect me because I know I'm not that type of lawyer.

- It doesn't impact my self-image, but I think it has had a very adverse effect on our profession. I think this effort to demonize lawyers is based on organizations that exist to destroy the right to a jury trial. It's a part of an organized plan to destroy the civil justice system. It isn't an accident or from a perception based on a few bad apples—it's due to corporate planning.
- I enjoy the humor as much as anyone else.
- I'm saddened for our profession because I think the greater community thinks far less of us than they think of car salesmen.
- I could care less.
- I'm a good lawyer so it doesn't bother me at all.
- I just laugh at those jokes along with everyone else.
- You have to pick on somebody, so it might as well be us. I've been around long enough that I have my own credibility in the community and in the Bar. Women now have a better shot at equal treatment.
- In spite of lawyer jokes, when I say I'm a lawyer, people look at me with respect, whether they're poor or wealthy, educated or not.
- Within the profession, we're so diligent about reinforcing the idea that we're in a privileged position and we have a responsibility to disprove these jokes and rumors. I'm surprised at the immediate social respect people give me when I tell them I'm an attorney. The negative reaction is in the minority.
- It doesn't impact my image because I know how lawyers are, the good and the bad. But it impacts the public's perception of us.
- People are interested to find out you're an attorney. They may have opinions on medical malpractice reform or workman's compensation, and have formed either good or bad opinions.

- In any profession, you'll have unprofessional people.
- Have you noticed that in the cartoons containing lawyer jokes, the lawyers are all men!

And some of the women shared their philosophical views on the whole "joking" matter:

- Lawyers really deserve a lot of respect. You can criticize and make nasty jokes about me, but when your ass is in a sling, I'll save your butt!
- We lawyers all kind of laugh about it. The judge is the one who makes decision. Our image is the same as a used car salesman or one rung lower. But when someone has hired a lawyer he's relied on, he'll say, "I liked my lawyer." Most people are actually very positive about their own experience with a lawyer, but the public image persists.
- I have met people who have a predisposition about lawyers because of previous bad experiences. But once they get to know you, it changes their opinions. I believe an attorney is in control of her own reputation. Attorneys will be ultimately judged for who they are and on their own merits.
- That's why lawyers get shot—because of those jokes. People forget that while lawyers were writing the Declaration of Independence, doctors were putting leeches on George Washington's ass!

While there is often a grain of truth in any negative humor—and there are attorneys who do behave as the jokes imply—the fact that lawyer jokes can actually make twenty percent of the interviewees ashamed to even admit that they are members of the legal profession is sad indeed. On the other hand, it is heartening to hear how some of the women go out of their way to counteract the negative impression of their chosen profession. Their proactive responses take them out of the role of "victims."

CHAPTER 5

WORKING WITH MALE ATTORNEYS

"What expectations do you think male attorneys have for a woman attorney that they may not have for a male attorney?" There's the good news—and the not-so-good news.

First, the good news. Six of the interviewees saw no differences between what male attorneys expect of female attorneys versus what they'd expect of another male lawyer.

- Once we have a dialogue going, most male attorneys are very respectful.
- I don't think the male lawyers in my practice area think any differently about male and female lawyers because our area is not adversarial.
- I'm in a collaborative area where male attorneys either initially or quickly see that there's no competence problem when they deal with me.
- I haven't found that men attorneys have any different expectations for me than they would for another male attorney. Although, one once said, "You're just being mean!"—and I don't think he'd say that to a male attorney!
- Some men still do have a stereotypical bias, others don't. Most people just consider your reputation as a lawyer regardless of your sex.
- They are savvy enough to understand that they'll be up against the same intellect, ambition, and drive that they

have. But competency is not gender-based. Some men I wouldn't let represent my dog!

And several interviewees add that male attorneys often have very positive expectations about working with female attorneys, as opposed to their male counterparts.

- My male partner perceives women as being less competitive and easier to get along with. He says there's an easier office dynamic with more women attorneys.
- They expect that you'll be nicer and more sensitive than their male counterparts. And some of my male colleagues are able to talk to me and express their feelings and frustrations, which is something they wouldn't be able to do it with a male—that old testosterone thing!
- They appreciate that they don't have to get into that male-butting-heads thing; they can drop their posturing and get to the point and not lose face.
- They assume that women attorneys will be more forgiving and less punitive.

But many of the interviewees' view male attorneys' expectations for women lawyers as negative, especially if those men are over fifty-years-old.

- It depends a lot on the generation. Men even ten years younger than I have a whole different perception from the guys who are fifty and older—who still show vestiges of the older attitudes that women attorneys are second class.
- Some think women lawyers need to be "honeyed up"—but they tend to be older guys. And some treat you like you're just a little less knowledgeable.
- I've only noticed a negative attitude toward women attorneys with older male attorneys.

- Male attorneys think we need to listen to them because they are older, wiser, and been around the block a lot more. They also expect that we will do exactly what they tell us to do.
- Older lawyers and baby boomers might have different expectations, but the current generation of men and women coming into the workforce are demanding a quicker track within the firm and work that is immediately meaningful. The older attorneys need to change if they're going to keep those bright minds.
- We're still not taken as seriously. Right now I'm dealing with a guy who graduated in the late fifties and still says, "Yes, dear," and is a little patronizing.

Younger male attorneys, however, are not off the hook. In sorting through the interviewees' comments, several negative themes occur.

THE "MOMMY" ISSUE

- A lot of male lawyers don't think it's possible to balance family life and business life. Subtly, I see men worry about what will happen when females start having kids—will they carry their weight? In firms, they go into a tizzy when women get pregnant and want to work half-time. Years ago they had no policy for maternity leave.
- They don't think you can juggle it all—work, life, and family. If you give more to your family than to your work, then there's an expectation that you're not a very good attorney.
- Men think women have limitations because women have children. They figure that a woman with kids won't be able to do a deposition.

- There's an expectation that you won't work as hard, and you won't work evenings or on the weekends.
- Some males think, "Is she a keeper, or is she going to do the "mommy" thing?"

TO BULLY—OR NOT?

- Some of them are shocked when they are dealing with a tenacious, unrelenting woman. They expect it will be easier to overwhelm women with the work they're putting out, the tone of their voice, or their physical size. They underestimate what they are dealing with!
- They think they can use more scare tactics on a woman—like getting in their faces. Once men attorneys have worked with women attorneys, they tend to expect us to be more prepared—because we usually are. They realize that we have to be taken seriously.
- Some still think women can be more easily bullied.
- Their perspectives are dichotomized: Either we're "bitches" if we're at all aggressive, or we're dumb "bitches." Some have yelled and screamed at me and called me stupid. You have to earn their respect.

HAVING TO PROVE ONESELF

- You still run into the man who feels you're just a half-inch above a secretary! Most guys expect women to be more touchy-feely and are surprised that you can calculate somebody's net worth. Of course, you can turn that to your advantage: If someone is being a "good old boy" and being a "rear end," I'll surprise them that I'm bright.
- Some of them just expect me to be a pushover.

- Men attorneys think we're not as bright, not as prepared. They interrupt me until they know me better. They seem surprised that I can do a nice job.
- A woman attorney has to prove herself more. There's a level of respect that needs to be earned by a woman to be on a par with male attorneys.
- Male attorneys think they can pull the wool over our eyes and manhandle us in negotiations and in the courtroom.
- Male attorneys expect us to be less aggressive.
- Some male attorneys still expect us to perform to a higher standard in order to prove ourselves.
- In the seventies, I had a male attorney who pulled my chair out in court because he didn't think I knew what I was doing. However, I had the evidence and I did prevail!
- I don't think we're taken as seriously. When I call a male attorney, they often return the call to my male partner!
- Sometimes male attorneys are raised to be more polite to women, which I sometimes use to my advantage. Before they know you, some male attorneys have expectations that you may not be quite as forceful or hard charging—and then they get surprised!
- There's still a tendency, especially in rural areas, to think that a woman attorney will be the sweet little lady who not be able to go toe-to-toe with them. A woman has to use her gender effectively and not try to be a man or men will think of her as a "bitch."
- The male attorney calls and says, "Got a minute? Will you go get the file? Now here's my response: On number 3, do this, etc." I tell them, "I'm not your secretary. Send it in writing." (I'm not talking about small changes, but major or expensive ones). Females wouldn't call a man and ask him to do that!

BEING EMOTIONAL

- They expect us to be more emotional about the presentation of our cases. If you get vehement in your argument, they think you're being too emotional. But they think you may fight a fairer fight than a man would.
- They worry that women attorneys will get emotional and won't be able to take the heat. They think you'll either cry or get shrew-like.
- Male attorneys expect women attorneys to be more organized—but also more emotional. They think it is more difficult to come to settlement because of a woman's orientation.
- They're scared to death they'll make us cry—either intentionally or unintentionally. They expect us not to be able to deal with criticism. If I'm hard to intimidate, don't cry, and I tell off-color jokes, they refer to me as "one of the guys."
- I've had older male lawyers tell me they're surprised that I'm not angry and emotional. It's a compliment.

One interviewee raised an issue about male attorneys' concerns about possible impropriety in working with a female attorney: "In my first practice group, I was with all men. One of the partners said, 'I can never put you on my litigation team because before a trial, we all go to a ranch to prepare. There would be a feeling of impropriety if I took you there.'"

A FINAL THOUGHT!

On a more philosophical note, one interviewee articulated her perception of male attorneys' relationships to their female colleagues this way: "Well, we don't have a penis, so we don't have to get into a contest about whose is bigger!"

CHAPTER 6

HOW ABOUT JUDGES?

When asked if they perceived differences in the way judges treat female and male attorneys, four interviewees felt they could not comment since they had no experience with litigation. Another thirteen (twenty-eight percent) flatly state that they see no difference at all. Asked the basis for this viewpoint, all remarked that judges expect respect, professionalism, and courtesy from both sexes—and treat both the same. One said, "I think judges have biases about new attorneys versus older ones, but it's not gender related."

Several interviewees make the point that judges did not treat women attorneys equally in the past, but do so now.

- For the most part, our judges are becoming pretty even handed. When I started out, both the Bench and the Bar represented an "old boys' club". It has changed over the years. Conscious efforts have been made for a more gender-balanced Bench. (In practice twenty-three years.)
- Early on we had judges who clearly thought women shouldn't be lawyers. I haven't seen that in recent years. (In practice thirty years.)
- In the past, there would have been a need for a woman to demonstrate competence. Not today, especially in probate court. (In practice twenty-nine years.)
- In today's world, judges are much more respectful than they were when I started—I see a big improvement. In

our state they got mandatory sensitivity training. (In practice nineteen years.)

- In one case, I was the plaintiff's attorney and the judge called us in to chambers before the hearing. He said he was not up to speed on the matter and needed a summary of the case—and he looked to the male attorney for it. I said, "I am the plaintiff's attorney." (In practice nineteen years.)
- At first, judges expected women to practice family law and not business law or high-end litigation. (In practice nineteen years.)
- It used not to be an equal playing field; now it is. (In practice twelve years.)
- It's getting better. For the most part, women are treated equally with male lawyers. There are some women judges who are older and expect you to have worked as hard to get up the ladder as they had to do, so sometimes they make it harder on you if you're younger and didn't have to work so hard to get where you are. (In practice nineteen years.)

Two interviewees think that differences do still exist in the way women are treated in court compared to their male counterparts—but only with older male judges.

- Older judges tend to think that females will be sweet, gentle, deferential, and non-aggressive.
- Older judges don't take women lawyers as seriously or give their arguments the credence they'd give to male, whom they see as a colleague.
- There's still gender bias in court. Older judges still call me "Missy."

Some interviewees cite isolated instances from the past in which they feel a judge had treated them differently.

- An older judge expected me to get him coffee and called me "Sugar Darling." (In practice six years.)
- A female judge asked that I be introduced as co-counsel when my male partner hadn't introduced me. (In practice fifteen years.)
- In 1979, I worked as a legal intern for a judge who said, "Why in the world would you want to be a lawyer?" (In practice twenty-six years.)
- When I was a brand new, a lawyer I was working for introduced me to a Superior Court female judge who addressed me as "little girl." My boss was there, so I didn't say anything—but it was part of the reason I moved out of the state a year later. (In practice seven years.)
- One trial judge refused to believe I was a lawyer and turned me away. (In practice forty years.)

However, forty percent of the interviewees continue to see differences in the way judges treat female attorneys. Their comments focus on expectations regarding appropriate dress in court, level of aggressiveness, being held to a higher standard, degree of preparation, and, lastly, the "Mommy issue".

APPROPRIATE DRESS

- I see some women attorneys who do not dress appropriately for court. They don't think the judge will have the balls to say something to a woman like they would to a man. One lady shows up in dirty pants, with her hair all disheveled and no jacket. Another appears as if she's going to a party and is all glittery. I find that a judge treats me more cordially because I show up in a dress or a skirt rather than pants.

- Some judges still demand that we wear skirts. Or they tell us that our voices are too high and we need to lower them—but if we tone it down, we're seen as meek.
- Always wear a skirt to court because most judges are a generation older and they see that as respectful. And judges are more likely to explain an objection to a female if you're respectful.
- Clothes in court can still be a problem. For men it's an easy uniform. But for women, the rules aren't as clear and some judges complain that women show too much cleavage or are too casual.
- Some judges expect women to wear panty hose and a dress, not pants.
- In court, I'm very sensitive about my shoes, hair and clothes. I keep my hair pulled back, not too sexy. The big issue now is whether or not to wear slacks to court—I won't do it. And some judges won't even allow it in their courts. There's also conflict about whether or not to wear hose.
- Once a judge said, "Oh, what a pretty suit—why don't you twirl around and show it to us? I just smiled, laughed a bit, shook my head, and said, 'Your Honor, we both know that would not be appropriate!'"

AGGRESSIVENESS

- Male judges have a gender expectation that you won't be as aggressive—yet if you act like a "bitch," you'll make them very uncomfortable.
- They expect us to be nicer—not to interrupt (although males do it all the time and get away with it).

- They think women should not be assertive—just get their point across and shut up. Even female judges let men argue their points a little longer.
- They expect a female attorney to be more polite. A judge once made a woman write a letter of apology to a witness—I can't imagine him requiring that of a man. Men can get away with bad conduct much easier than females.
- Judges expect women to fight among themselves less. Sometimes judges are too dismissive of women—they will describe her as "shrill" but not give a derogatory name to a man's sarcastic voice tone. Sometimes you'll still be called "Hon."

A HIGHER STANDARD

- We have a lot of women judges here, and they tend to expect that women will be prepared, organized, and be up-front with the court, which is a compliment. Because they had to come up the hard way, you'd better be competent too!
- I have no problem with male judges. But sometimes, the female judges are tougher on female attorneys. They seem to have higher expectations for us.
- Judges are going to expect a more rational, well-balanced argument—with the connection between facts and the law woven into a story format. Women piece the puzzle together better. But judges expect more emotion and a more circuitous argument from a woman.
- They cut women less slack.
- They expect women to have their fingers on the document or case, but will cut the guys a little more slack—"Oh, your secretary was out sick."

- In court, the winning lawyer typically will draft the order. But many times, they expect me to draft the order or do the more secretarial stuff.

BETTER PREPARATION

- I've heard judges say that women are often well prepared when they come to court, whereas men often wait until trial to prepare.
- Judges perceive women as more prepared in court because they have to make up with brains what they don't have in brawn. And you'd better have all your ducks in a row.
- Judges just expect women attorneys to be more prepared.

THE "MOMMY ISSUE"

- Judges are not going to give women a pass because of a need to re-arrange a schedule due to a non-emergency kid issue. This is a real challenge for women—they can easily seem not quite as committed when they do this type of rescheduling.
- Some judges are harder on female attorneys—like when they won't let a pregnant woman attorney take a bathroom break.
- The majority of time they expect us to be like the male attorneys. Many judges want to run a trial past five or six o'clock, which is horrible for single moms.

FINAL THOUGHTS

A few interviewees had very specific examples of differing expectations by judges for female attorneys.

- Judges expect women to use more family or personal examples in their closings.
- I've noticed that men will often be addressed by their first names, while women are addressed by their last names (or "counselor").
- In one case, there were lots of lawyers and I was the only woman. The judge would say, "Gentlemen, are we ready to proceed?" After the fourth day I said, "I must be dressing really funny for you to think I'm a gentleman!" This angered him, and for the rest of his tenure as judge he would exaggerate and say, "Gentlemen and Mizzzzzzzzz."
- There's the problem of sexual harassment that occurs with judges (and with law firm senior partners), which sometimes includes blatant sexual joking. The most common form is a quid-pro-quo: "Sleep with me and you'll get ..." or "Let's have dinner—I'm sure I can help you out."

CHAPTER 7

WOMAN TO WOMAN

How do the women attorneys perceive their relationships with other women attorneys? Do they expect better treatment from other women than they might expect when dealing with their male colleagues?

Interestingly, about thirty-five percent of the interviewees felt that their interactions with other women lawyers were likely to be negative due to increased aggressiveness and competitiveness.

- Some woman attorneys tend to fall on the aggressive side because they had to survive: "Let me pounce on you, intimidate the hell out of you, see what you do, and then I'll react." If they're older, it's more, "Listen, I've been doing this for a long time—you need to listen to me!"
- I expect other females to work with me on the level, and not be dirty or conniving. With one female attorney (my same age and practice length), I expected mutual respect and decorum in the courtroom. When we see each other socially, she's very pleasant. But in the courtroom, she's very dirty. She should know that's not the way to treat other attorneys, especially female attorneys.
- I expect other female attorneys to be "bitchy."
- Women are just as mean to women. There's not a whole lot of "I want to help you up." You pay your own dues. There's no cutting you any slack. And older women lawyers don't stick their necks out for younger women lawyers.

- Women attorneys may be giving more credit to men attorneys. Generally, the better attorneys I've run into have been men, but they've been doing it longer and have mentors. Many women go into practice without ever practicing with a firm and not having mentors, which is a clear mistake.
- I don't expect as much of a woman lawyer. She's probably thinking, "Are you a "bitch?"
- Early in my practice, I felt I had a higher expectation for ethics and professionalism. The first time a female attorney didn't meet those expectations, I felt so betrayed. It happens a lot.
- Some women lawyers are very competitive with other women lawyers—more so than with men.
- On occasion, a woman may expect you to cut her some slack because you're in the sisterhood. And you may run into one who doesn't expect the same kind of relentlessness because some people think that's a male characteristic.
- There can be competition with another female, which can make things more difficult. One lawyer I know does things that are over the edge, and she expects me to cut her some slack because she's a woman. Sometimes I won't take a case because of hard feelings with the woman on the other side.
- Unfortunately, sometimes stereotypes are true. Some women do not like strong, hard women attorneys; they're seen as dragon ladies, bulldogs, "bitches," etc. But a man can be like that, too—and that's not good either. The issue is professionalism in general.
- Some women attorneys still think women are less qualified than their male counterparts.

- There are two different types of women attorneys. Some are very competitive and expect other women to undermine them. Others expect other women to help them.
- Women tend to be more competitive when working with women.
- I've come across a number of female attorneys who have such low self-esteem that they pump themselves up by being jerks.
- With some, the first phone call and they're screaming at me. I had a female lawyer try to slap me, and then she threw a pen in my face.

But the majority of interviewees (sixty-five percent) had positive things to say about their expectations of treatment from other women attorneys. Their comments revolve around a mutual expectation of women's cooperative relationship skills, and of their competence and capability.

COOPERATION AND RELATIONSHIP SKILLS

- Women attorneys start out thinking that there should be a bond on some level with another female attorney. We expect one another to be more open and more professional. We're going to communicate and not try to stab one another in the back. If I need an extra day, she'll give me one!
- Sometimes—especially if you're a litigator—women expect other women to be more cooperative and to meet deadlines.
- Women lawyers have more personal relationships with one another and vent to one another. That fosters our confiding in one another.

- I always expect more courtesy from women. I'm always shocked and betrayed when a woman treats me like a guy lawyer would—like an enemy.
- I expect other women attorneys to be more even-tempered and more open to my proposals or ideas.
- Women attorneys think that maybe a women attorney will be nicer.
- Women attorneys expect more collegiality from their peers.
- We expect other women attorneys to be ethical. And we have to recognize that we'll be practicing together for years to come and that we need to keep good rapport with one another.
- We generally expect another woman attorney to be more pleasant to deal with.
- Women attorneys expect other women attorneys to visit more—to have time to stop by and chat. Men think that too—that you can drop by and chat with a woman and she won't mind.
- We expect more emotionality from one another. And better organization. And better settlements.
- We expect a little more compassion and a little less aggression from one another.
- Women attorneys expect that they'll be able to get along and trust one another. I don't always feel you can trust the other side if a male is opposing counsel. You assume that a woman will be fair, not jack around and play games. I know a woman attorney who lies, and people who know her think all women attorneys lie, unfortunately.
- I expect woman attorneys to be more sensible. We don't expect the egos and the posturing that we find with male attorneys. We talk like reasonable human beings.

- We can have a more frank discussion with less posturing. With other women you can say, "Gee, I didn't understand that—can you please explain?" or "I have a question." Men have trouble saying, "I don't know."
- Women attorneys expect to get along on a case. We can work it out rather than escalating with motions back and forth. We have more empathy and kinship with other women in the law profession.

CAPABILITY AND COMPETENCE

- I expect women colleagues to be smart and thoughtful in their arguments, and to understand when it's time to cut the advocacy part and look for the merits of a case so we can settle more quickly.
- We expect that women will do a better job. If you care about your client and you refer them to a woman, she'll be more thorough and pay more attention to a client's needs.
- Women have higher expectations for female colleagues than for males. Women have to prove themselves more.
- Maybe women expect their female colleagues to be a little bit more professional. We hold each other to a higher standard because we're women.
- I expect most women to be a little more detail oriented.
- I expect women attorneys to act in a more professional manner and to be prepared so they aren't making other women look bad. I have to be overly prepared, and I expect other women to do the same thing.
- We have expectations for other women attorneys that we have for ourselves—that we're capable and can get the job done. Our expectations for other women may be higher than for men—that you should do more to prove yourself and work harder.

- We're harder on ourselves; we have higher expectations of competence.
- I expect women attorneys to be pretty sharp. I want them to do well—and to be fair.
- I always want other women to be really good at being an attorney. I kind of expect them to be. Getting through law school is still more difficult than for a man. We will reach equality when a mediocre woman has as much chance for success as a mediocre man—and we're not there yet.

FINAL THOUGHTS

Some interviewees expressed more philosophical comments about working with other female attorneys.

- Some think we "girls" will or should stick together. But gender doesn't trump firm loyalty.
- The thought processes in females are different: We have a tendency to be circular and men are more linear.
- Women lawyers have the expectation that women can juggle it all. We expect to keep our careers going, yet make sure our families are taken care of. If you give more to your family than to work, then there is perhaps an expectation that you're not a good attorney.
- We're all in this together. A lot of women in committees expect other women to vote for the female, regardless of her qualifications, in order to advance women in general. I think we need to vote for the females!
- We all have the same interests; we're all on the same page. That's true, but doesn't necessarily mean we'll all get along. Sometimes people think we all have the same viewpoint just because we're all women!

CHAPTER 8

THAT ELUSIVE LIFE BALANCE

One of the most significant ways that professional women differ from their male counterparts has to do with their lives outside of work. Whether married or single, women are more likely to have the major responsibilities of caring for children and elderly parents, and running a household, all in addition to tending to their careers.

Here's what the interviewees say about their stresses in managing a wide variety of roles.

THE STRESS OF BEING A PARENT

- Even though I have a very supportive husband, I still carry the primary responsibility for the family. You know, the laborious part of raising kids: doctor's appointments, taking off work when the kids are sick, buying the kids' clothes.
- When your kids are young, you have to play more roles and can't be as focused on your career as a man can.
- Doing everything is difficult for a woman. If you want to have a family, society has different expectations for you.
- By choice, women are still taking the majority of the home responsibilities, especially the childrearing. If the kids get sick, the woman is expected to leave the office. Husbands do things when it pleases them and we women do it because somebody has to. My women friends

who are attorneys do all the work at home; we have trouble letting go.

- I feel the pressures of home life and children more than my husband does. I have to have a separation between work and home. I can't have the kids at my office, so I'm the default person when my kids are sick.
- We just have to balance family priorities more than men have to.
- Most male litigators have a spouse that stays home and takes care of the family needs. That isn't true for women, especially if you're a single mom.
- It's different for women because we have the children. So there still has to be the tradeoff; maybe more hours at night—doing a brief at ten or eleven o'clock. A guy can go to sleep but the woman has other obligations. There's always a lack of time because you're doing two different jobs; the guys have more time to network or to go to early morning meetings.
- If you have kids, it requires better organization and balance.

One interviewee without children still recognizes the enormous pressures that come with parenting: "Because I'm single with no children, I don't have the same pressures and expectations as most of my female attorney friends. I don't know how they do it."

THE STRESS OF MULTIPLE ROLES

- I have to be better than a man—not so much in the legal aspects—but better about juggling the many roles I play. I'm lucky because I have an extended family who helps and a husband who is a "wife." Women have to figure out all aspects of our entire lives and men don't have to do that.

- Traditionally and by their own choice, women have more tasks than men—they take on more roles. I try to be a caretaker, housekeeper, decorator, cook, wife, mom, etc.
- I think female lawyers have more challenges with home life than males.
- Though more and more men are looking for balance in their lives, women still feel far more of the responsibility for keeping relationships going, for home and hearth. It doesn't matter if they have kids or not; if they don't have them, it just means fewer people to feel guilty about. There's still a great deal of guilt and anxiety about being all you can be in all of your roles.
- I think most women have many more responsibilities than most men. You have to be willing to balance well and sacrifice.
- The women I know in a law practice still have the responsibility for their home lives, so they have to juggle more.

With all this stress, it becomes imperative to find a family-friendly firm, which, according to one interviewee, is a real challenge. One woman talks of her experience in a firm that treats women with children differently than the men in the firm. "If I leave work at a reasonable time, the firm pegs me as on the 'mommy track' and I'm not perceived as a serious lawyer. But if a guy leaves at a reasonable time, people think, 'Oh, isn't that great! He's interested in his kids!' and he is not perceived as less dedicated."

One interviewee expresses a somewhat different viewpoint. She feels that women should know the kind of firm culture they are joining and not complain about it. "Be willing to take responsibility for the choices you make. Like them or change them, but don't whine!"

Interestingly, when asked what one question they'd have for other women attorneys, the majority of the interviewees said they'd like to know more about how the other women handle the juggling of their many roles. None feel that they have yet mastered the art of life/career balance. Clearly, this work/life balance issue is their biggest frustration. Yet in spite of acknowledging that they are not even close to having "all the answers," the women still were willing to provide their own "best tip" for balancing career and home life. They involve re-working one's expectations, having other interests besides work, setting clear priorities, creating a support structure, and implementing practice management procedures that facilitate life balance.

REALISTIC EXPECTATIONS

The "you-can-have-it-all" mindset can create some unrealistic expectations. Remedy: A heavy dose of reality.

- Do the best you can and realize that you can't do it all and you can't do it perfectly. I used to think I could!
- Accept something less than perfection. Allow your house to go to ruins because it really doesn't matter. Get a cleaning lady and a nanny if you can. Get a support system. Look into getting a concierge service.
- Somebody once said, "Life isn't always 50/50." You can't feel guilty if your life is ninety percent work one week. Take advantage when you do have more time for your family. You don't have to do everything. If you have dust bunnies under the bed, live with them!
- You need to look objectively at what you have to get done, rather than what your type-A personality thinks you have to get done.

WORK ISN'T EVERYTHING!

For many interviewees, a key to maintaining work-life balance is to make sure they spend time doing things other than working or thinking about their work.

- I am careful to make sure that I am active in things outside of law. I need to associate with others who are not related to my law practice.
- Work hard, but then leave work behind. Make plans each week for other non-lawyer things, like being with friends and family. You have to actively plan it.
- Get lots of exercise. Don't be afraid to admit that you need help because you're afraid you'll look weak.
- I safeguard my private time. I'd rather work late than take work home.
- Try to confine your work to work hours and make sure when you go home that you're spending time doing things with your family. Knock off at 5 or 5:30 p.m., and go home. Write things down so you don't forget about them.
- Don't let yourself be identified by your job. Use the Rule of Twelve: When you leave the office, you have to wait at least twelve hours before you come back!
- Leave your work at the office and leave your home life at home. You have to separate the two. Try to fit your practice around your life and around what makes you happy. Don't do things you don't like to do. Focus on what makes you most satisfied.
- Maintain good friendships outside of your profession—it gives you more balance. With friends you are able to be yourself without expectations. Maintain a good sense of humor; we take ourselves too seriously. We expect so much more of ourselves than men expect of themselves.

- If you don't have children, have an animal or a hobby—whatever floats your boat. Have some activity that relaxes you—a book club or a supper club. Do something every day that takes you away from the law, or you'll be a totally boring person.
- Set your boundaries early on. Figure out what you need to do to keep sane, whether it is exercising, taking work home with you, whatever. Protect yourself.
- Create the time to quit thinking about work.
- I have to schedule quality time with my husband to keep our relationship alive (as well as time with the kids). I don't keep any secrets from him, which I think is important. I'm very open with my husband about what I'm doing because men can be jealous.
- It's also important not to get so caught up in work that you lose touch with your interests and the people you care about—it's hard to get those relationships.
- Remember that work is just that—work. Schedule an hour a day to work out or to have time for yourself. Just don't get too wrapped up in your work.
- Try to set regular hours and not take work home with you—but it's almost impossible!
- Develop some sort of ritual when you leave the office in the afternoon that disengages you from work. There's a danger in that you can take on your clients' problems as your own. When I get in the car, I listen to my favorite music—not the news. I don't want to hear horror stories; I want to calm down and get into a different mental space.

PRIORITIES, PLEASE!

Other interviewees talk about the importance of having clear priorities, and then sticking to them.

- Pick your priorities and set your goals accordingly. Spend more time with your children, and make monetary issues secondary.
- Work to live; don't live to work! Your family is your priority. Love what you do, but don't make it your number one priority. Your inbox should always be full.
- Be able to compartmentalize. Don't let your daily life at home interfere with your work—and the other way around.
- You have to put your priorities up front and center. Controlling your schedule is part of it. The other part is to hire as much help as you possibly can. There are delegatable and non-delegatable duties. Cleaning house is infinitely delegatable, being at your child's recital is not. Forget about who is doing the cleaning and the dishes, and maintain your relationship with your husband or significant other.
- Understand what your priorities are and don't place yourself in a situation where they can't be met. Otherwise, you'll constantly be disappointed.
- You've got to figure out what the expectations are at home first. I intentionally got pregnant my first year of law school so any firm would know that family is important to me. You've got to get your home life squared away first. It is very doable—to have a great practice and a great family life.
- Try to fit your practice around your life and around what makes you happy. Don't do things you don't like to do. Focus on what makes you most satisfied.
- From week to week, things change both professionally and in your home life. I'm always dedicating more time to one than another, though I try to keep family as my main priority.

- Get a really clear handle on your priorities. Make sure they include both home and work, and then keep an eye on which needs to dominate. And keep your sense of humor.

SUPPORT HELPS

One interviewee created support for herself by having her parents live a half a block from her house "so they could pitch in with my girls." But for others, key support comes from their significant others.

- It helps to marry the right person!
- My husband is always ready to pitch in.
- Marry someone who will do the laundry, the dishes, the shopping, and who will help with the kids. Decide what things you want to trade off on. For example, for a long time I never read novels. I didn't do as much marketing as I might have if I didn't have kids. And don't even ask me about TV shows!
- Choose the right life partner!
- Have a supportive spouse; in other words, get a husband who'll be a "wife"!

PRACTICE MANAGEMENT TIPS

Many interviewees give suggestions about managing their practices in such a way as to maximize life balance.

- Don't say yes to every client who walks in the door. Determine when something is truly an emergency that should come before your family. Don't be misled by the client who wants something filed *today* just to show someone up.
- You need to hire very good staff and delegate whatever you can.

- Learn the importance of screening out whom you work with as clients. This makes a difference in your quality of life.
- Get a Practice Management Coach!
- Block time on your calendar for family and personal time just like you would a client appointment. Have your receptionist call it a "meeting"—not "She went to the hairdresser," or "She went home to be with her husband."
- Two things: First, you have to set a schedule for yourself and stick to it. If you say you'll be at the office Mondays, Wednesdays, and Fridays and are not there, it breeds a misperception that you're not that committed to your work. Second, set your limits and clearly communicate what they are.
- Part of it is educating employers to have flexible arrangements. Larger firms are becoming more sensitive to keeping good females on board with "mommy tracks" and daycares. You have to push for those things if you want balance.
- Establish boundaries with your clients. Don't care about them so much that you allow them to call you about silly issues at all hours of the day and night.
- At the office, treat your personal life like a client needing attention. Just say, "I have an appointment." You don't need to say whom it's with or where it is!
- Just focus on whatever deserves the most attention on any given day.
- Be able to explain your priorities to your clients and to your family. For example, my clients know that during the school month I'm out the door at a certain time because I want to help my kids with their homework. But there's a trade-off—clients know that I'll speak with them after 9 p.m. once my kids are in bed. And my kids

know that I have to go to court sometimes, which means that I won't be able to meet them coming off the bus.

- Just force yourself to do what you need to do to get things done, but don't overdo it. You have to pace yourself and not be the one in the office at 10 o'clock at night.
- I won't take more than a certain number of custody cases at once because I want balance in my life.
- You need to leave the office when 5 or 6 o'clock rolls around. Work will always be there. If you don't take care of yourself, you can't help your clients.

One interviewee found that working part-time was a good solution: "I worked part time when I was raising my kids, which was unheard of at that time. Men thought I wasn't committed to my career and that I wouldn't be successful. When I didn't have a trial I would leave at noon, but I worked a lot at home."

A REAL SOLUTION?

Finally, one interviewee is very clear about her solution to the work-life balance issue:

- Give up housekeeping! It just doesn't matter what all the magazines say. You can't have it all; you have to pick what's most important. Let go of some of those expectations. If your house basically is clean and your kids are fed, you've accomplished what you need to at home. We eat salads and sandwiches—or we eat the same thing two nights in a row. My daughter went on a trip to Mexico to study Spanish, and the woman with whom she lived made a wonderful alphabet soup that my daughter loved. When the woman gave my daughter the recipe, my daughter responded with, "That's so nice of you, but my mother doesn't cook!" The woman gasped and clutched her throat!

CHAPTER 9

GEMS OF WISDOM

For any female attorney beginning her career—or for women thinking about entering the legal profession—wouldn't it be great to hear some practical advice from women lawyers who have "been there, done that"? Here's what these women had to say.

CHOOSE YOUR PRACTICE AREA CAREFULLY

- Law in general is like having a bachelor's degree—there are so many things you can do with it. So find what you love. Don't be a mile wide and an inch deep. Find a specialty. Know yourself and find a practice area that lets you be that person.
- If your home life matters—and eventually, it will!—pick your practice area carefully. Litigation is hard on family life. In-house work is a good solution; it keeps your hours down.
- Understand what you are looking for. To give yourself the best odds of accomplishing your goal, target what you do and where you do it. For example, if you want children, to be a partner, and work hours from nine to five, then don't go into a firm that doesn't operate that way. You can't rail against an employer for not having the same goals as you do.
- Read everything you can about your area of practice and hone your writing skills so they are impeccable.

- Find an area of practice with which you are comfortable.
- Figure out your personal style. If you're not the cut-throat litigator type, then don't go into that field. Figure out what you do best and look for a job in law that takes advantage of your unique skills.
- You have to know yourself, your goals, and your aspirations—in terms of time, money, the kind of practice you want. Law is a profession that is very status conscious. It starts with the Law Review in law school. Then you have to go to a "good" firm. I left the Law Review because it was run more as a hazing process than a learning process, and I was told that leaving it would be the end of my career—but it wasn't so.
- Maintain your confidence and don't just take any job. Take the job that allows you to maintain a healthy and sane lifestyle. And don't go get the coffee for the boss all the time!
- Think about what you want to accomplish in your life. There are many different areas and ways to practice law. Really think about your goals and priorities. Don't get caught up in the have-to-work-for-the-biggest-firm-and-make-the-most-money trap. Think about your career long-term.
- Recognize that you have lots of options open to you as an attorney.
- You need to know yourself very well and not assume that the area of law you think you'll be best at is the right one. Experience a wide variety of situations to see where you'll flourish. And don't take anything personally because all that BS that goes on in a law firm isn't really about you.
- Focus on what type of law you would gain the most satisfaction from and steer your career in that direction.

Think about the hours that will be involved and how the practice works.

- Find out what part of law you want to work in. If you're not sure, work at a state or government agency, or a public defender or prosecutor's office where you can try cases and get a feel for what kinds of cases you like. Get a job in a courtroom learning how to try a case. Get to know judges and lawyers well and you'll benefit from that network, which you can rely on later.

GET MENTORED

- Find a good mentor to work with you, to support you and to talk to you about your practice.
- Find one or more people whom you admire and respect to be your mentor. I'm shocked by how so many lawyers haven't had them. I've taken so many bits and pieces from different mentors to be the person I am today. If there's nobody that comes to mind in your firm, go somewhere else.
- Many senior women attorneys will be eager to help you if you just reach out to them.
- Get your first job with a reasonably-sized firm. Get with someone who knows how to practice law well and learn the ropes.
- Study the people you work around or see in a courtroom, and then work for them and emulate them. But you have to be you and find your own style.
- Find a good mentor to work with you, to support you, and to talk to you about your practice.
- Do an internship with a law firm; do it for free if you have to. As an intern, you can ask to be hands-on in cases and in dealing with clients. Make sure you find

yourself a therapist on the side or somebody to talk to. You'll need a place to vent to deal with all the angst.

FOSTER GOOD RELATIONSHIPS

- Be realistic and understand that you're going to forge relationships with other attorneys—so always stay professional and you'll have an easier time practicing in the future.
- For new lawyers, make yourself indispensable to your clients and your partners. Learn everything you can about a case, but think about it creatively. Don't just do a narrow assignment, but think about how other issues apply. Offer ideas. Stay conscious about your interactions with others. You have to play politics a bit differently.
- We don't have to win every argument or get everything right to be effective. Sometimes we push so hard that we lose sight of the battle and the true goal. Build good relationships with your peers—that's huge—good personal relationships. And good relationships with clients can save them lots of money.
- When I clerked for a judge, her secretary told me to talk to my assistant and tell her what I need from her and ask her what she needs from me. Working out a good relationship with an assistant is critical—because they can kill you if they want to.

REFUSE TO BE INTIMIDATED

- Don't be intimidated. If you can pass the Bar, don't let anyone put anything over on you.
- Sometimes, you may not feel as smart because you're not on Wall Street. But I've been with big firms and those lawyers aren't any better or smarter than people in smaller towns. Once some high-powered attorneys

drove into our small town in limos with professional drivers and charged $850 an hour. I charged $250 and found out that they knew less than I did.

- Don't be intimidated. Work hard, be honest—and be clear with the other attorneys in your office about what role you expect to play.
- Be confident. But it's the hardest thing!
- Toughen up! A judge once told me why he thinks men are better litigators. Boys are encouraged to play sports like football. In football, your team gets slaughtered and it is humiliating. Women tend to quit. You have to be able to lose and be tough.

BE TRUE TO YOURSELF

- Be yourself. Be prompt. Be professional. Be personable. Being outgoing has worked for me.
- Be yourself. In law school I discovered that by the time some women graduated they tried to clone themselves to be like men—they even wore ties and crisp suits, and cut their hair. I think there's a special place in the law for women and I purposefully wear a pretty pin or scarf to show my gender. I'm proud of my gender. This is a people profession, not a male profession, and it is important to maintain your femininity.
- Always act with integrity and be true to yourself.
- Have a really clear idea about your strengths—and then play to those.

MAINTAIN YOUR PROFESSIONALISM

- Be consistent and be ethical.

- Be professional and honor your commitments. One of my concerns with women attorneys is that they use "family comes first" as an excuse. When a deposition or something else in a busy practice demands her attendance and she says, "My kid is sick today"—that doesn't cut it. She needs to arrange—or re-arrange—things on the home front so she can do her job.
- You often only have one chance to make a good impression and build your reputation, so make it a good one. Don't be catty; keep it professional. When we start talking differently, then maybe that's when we're treated differently.

STRIVE FOR BALANCE

- Find activities in addition to law that you really enjoy and become very involved in them, whatever they are. This will help you build your business and give you an outlet so you can balance your life. At the same time, you must work in a dedicated way on your career. There is no short cut to being a good lawyer.
- Keep a balance. Know what you want to achieve in your practice so you can achieve your goals, but maintain a balance with the quality of your life outside the firm.
- There is always a way to balance what you want to have personally and professionally—you will only be limited by your creativity, or lack of it. Think of that Lladró piece with the woman holding a briefcase with the child in front holding a book bag. Be flexible. My schedule has changed many times over the past ten years to accommodate family changes
- Try to achieve life balance early on—and then keep it!

PAY YOUR DUES

- I had to work long hours to get where I have. Pay your dues the first five years. But don't lose sight of the things that are important in life even when you are paying those dues.
- Wear the navy blue suits even though you can't stand them. It takes about five years to realize that you're real, so be patient with yourself while you're still a baby lawyer.

FOLLOW YOUR BLISS

- Only be good at doing what you love. If you find yourself in a law firm doing things you hate, get out—find your own place. Many women are leaving the profession or go into their own practices or government service.
- It's simple. Do what you love!

AND SOME FINAL THOUGHTS

- Definitely maintain a sense of humor at all costs. Know that the first years are difficult, but it gets better. You have to work really hard to be good at your profession, so resign yourself to it. Stand up for yourself; you have to be assertive.
- Read the book *Women Don't Ask* by Babcock and Laschever. It's about negotiation and the gender divide. The premise is that women don't ask for as much as readily as men do. Yet women's negotiating and compromising skills are much better than what men have.
- Be prepared. It's everything in practicing law.
- Respect your time and make sure you get paid for what you do. Women are often raised to put the wellbeing and care of other people first, so they don't take care of the

money end of their practice. I've seen many women go under as a result.

- Just focus on your practice and work hard.
- If a woman is planning on having children, take a breather—or a job that is less demanding—until the kids are four or five. This would save a lot of hardship.
- It is important to start every day with a smile and tell yourself that you can do it. Your staff will be a reflection of you. If staff is not working out, get rid of them sooner rather than later. Same thing with a client: If I have a bad feeling about them, I trust it and don't take them on.
- Don't make a big deal out of being female. Just do your best at what you do and be respected as an attorney.
- Don't focus on the negative; no "poor me." Look at what you can appreciate about your practice. For example, I had cancer and had to dump everything in my office for a time. So many attorneys came to help me with my files; yet there were a few who used the situation as an opportunity to steal business. I prefer to focus on all the people who helped.

CHAPTER 10

SOME THOUGHTS FROM A PRACTICE MANAGEMENT COACH

It is clear from these fifty women attorneys' responses that issues of discrimination faced by women going into the law profession a decade or two ago have declined in recent years. Overall, women feel less of a need to have to "prove themselves" as competent before they are given the respect due them. Exceptions appear primarily when women are younger and just starting to practice, when they are litigators in large firms and when they are dealing with older males (whether clients, judges, or male attorneys).

Given their frustrations in having practices that fulfill their original expectations, it is imperative that women be given practical, realistic information about what practicing law is really like. Ideally, this would happen before they decide to enter law school—but certainly merits discussion while in law school.

What information would be desirable?

WHAT SIZE FIRM?

The pros and cons of firms' size need to be made clear. From the interviewees' reports, many of them (and their women attorney peers) started out in larger firms, but then opted to go it alone, or with another attorney or two, because of the large firm cultures. They valued the learning and experience they received from the large firms, but wanted more freedom and independence.

It is commonly known that larger law firms are having difficulty retaining their new hires. Female lawyers, in particular, tend to leave their firms after three years— for solo practice or to join with colleagues in small firms of two to ten attorneys. Since lawyers coming out of law school spend their first few years in a large firm being mentored and trained, the firms don't begin getting a financial return on their investments until those new lawyers have worked four or five years. With the increasing exodus after three years, the large firms are losing money. The old model is broken. With an average of forty-eight percent of law school graduates in the last five years being women, the problem is significant.

Of course, not all large firms are the same; many are changing their policies in order to be more attractive to women. At the very least, before making a decision to join a firm, women need to talk with other women in that firm to get a sense of what it's really like to work there.

WHICH PRACTICE AREA?

Given that women still feel they bear the larger share of responsibility for family and home life issues, it would be most helpful to know the differences in lifestyle expectations and client issues for lawyers who practice in the various areas of law. Transactional attorneys generally have an easier time with "life balance" than do litigators. Family, estate planning, and elder law attorneys often deal with more emotional client issues—a personality fit for some lawyers, but not for others. Once an attorney (or potential one) has narrowed down her choice of practice areas to two or three, she can schedule a lunch with several attorneys who are already practicing in those areas to "pick their brains" about the pros and cons of those particular types of practices.

By understanding the typical lifestyles of women practicing in a particular area of law, as well as their own personal goals (including whether or not they plan to have children), a woman hopefully can make an informed choice of a practice area that will be a better fit for her individual circumstances. Counselors, teachers, and mentors need to encourage women to consider life goals as well as career goals.

THE BUSINESS SIDE

Because so many women opt out of the large firms due to concerns about family obligations, information on running the business of a law practice would be very valuable. Setting up one's own practice requires much more than just knowledge of the law and the technical skills that are learned in law school. Suddenly, an attorney has to be her own marketer, human resource person, bookkeeper, bill collector, customer service representative, and administrator (larger firms typically provide such services). Information on how to recruit, hire, and retain staff would be invaluable, as would guidelines on law firm financials and budgeting.

A FINAL QUESTION—AND SOME ANSWERS!

Remember the final interview question asked of all the women: "If you had one question that you would like to ask other women attorneys, what would it be?" Almost all said they wanted more information on how other women attorneys meet their "life balance" challenges. Clearly, this is the area where huge stress can occur.

Since my work as a Practice Management Coach for attorneys almost always includes this "life balance" dilemma (even with male attorneys!), I'd like to end this book by sharing some tips that my clients have found helpful in creating law practices that serve their lives rather than having lives that serve their practices. Though "life balance" is an ideal that may take continual striving to accomplish, it all boils down to setting priorities, combined with good time management.

WRITE YOUR PERSONAL AND PROFESSIONAL MISSION STATEMENTS

Though you might tend to think of this as a "blow off" assignment and want to skip over it, don't! Think about it: What could be more helpful than giving careful thought to the kind of life you want to have—both personally and career-wise? Spending an hour or so in personal reflection about this establishes clarity. And often, figuring out what it is that you really want is the hardest part!

For your personal mission statement, jot down some ideas about what part of the country you want to live in and what kind of home environment you desire. What kind of family life and friendships do you plan to have? What types of recreation do you enjoy? How important is health and fitness to your lifestyle? What hobbies, passions, and interests do you need to consider? How involved do you want to be in your community and in various organizations? What about your spiritual development?

In your professional mission statement, consider the kind of practice area you want, the size of firm that will best fit your needs, your financial goals, and the type of office environment you want to create. What will be your business philosophy? Your core values?

Having these mission statements and projecting ahead into your future helps get you focused and clear. As you begin your practice of law—or decide to re-engineer the practice you have —you may as well begin thinking *now* about creating the kind of practice that you'll want to have ten, twenty, or thirty years from now.

SET "SMART" GOALS

Once you've established your mission statements, goal-setting becomes easier. Just take each concept in those statements and ask yourself, "Where do I want to be on this aspect of my life ten years from now?" And then in five years? And then in one year? Working backwards from year ten to year one helps you to keep the bigger picture in mind. If ten years out seems impossible to think about, go for five years, three years, and then one year.

Remember to use the "SMART" Goals acronym. "S" is for "specific." "I want to lose weight" is not specific. "I want to lose five pounds a month for six months" is specific. "I want to get more control of my time" is not specific." "I will block out a minimum of two hours per day for production" is specific.

"M" is for "measurable." How are you going to measure your results to know if you accomplished the goal? For example, if your goal is to do marketing lunches twice a week, the measurement would be seeing those lunches scheduled on your calendar. "I'm going to delegate document preparation to my paralegal" would be measured by noting what documents were prepared by the paralegal.

The "A" involves "action." Does the goal have action(s) associated with it? A goal "to be friendlier" doesn't state what you're going to actually do in order to be friendlier; "I'm going to have lunch with one friend a week" does. ""I'm going to have a staff meeting every Monday at 9" is an action item that can be calendared.

"R" is for "realistic." Is it really possible for you to achieve this goal? Losing thirty pounds in a month is probably unrealistic—not to mention unhealthy. To plan a large marketing event for your firm in a week in which a big trial is scheduled is probably not very realistic.

Finally, "T" is for "timeline." Your goal must have a stated time for completion. Having a deadline keeps you moving forward and provides accountability. With larger projects, you may need to set a series of timelines in order to make sure that the final result occurs at the time you've planned.

Admittedly, there is quite a bit of work in setting goals for the next decade. But once you've done it, it's easy to take your one-year goals and break them down to ninety days—and then, finally, the next thirty-day goals. You'll revise the ninety-day goals every ninety days and, using those, the thirty-day goals every thirty days. With your thirty-day goals, you have something practical to work with on a daily basis.

Keep your thirty-day professional goals in a prominent place in your office—on the top of your inbox, in the front of your day timer, on the wall in front of your telephone, as wallpaper on your computer screen—anywhere that allows you to see them every day. With your thirty-day personal goals, you might put them on your bathroom mirror, your closet door, or on a bulletin board by your home telephone—again, anywhere where you will see them frequently.

Why does this form of goal-setting help with life balance? Because it gives you a clarity of direction, a sense of purpose and, most of all, a focus that is based on a carefully thought out plan to get you where you really want to be in your life.

ORGANIZE YOUR OFFICE

If you have piles of files—on your desk, your credenza, perhaps your floor—you may not think it's a problem (other than having to take clients into a conference room so they won't see the clutter). And you may believe that you know where everything is in those piles (studies show that it's just not true). Even if you're correct, the biggest problem with clutter is the psychological feeling of being overwhelmed that results from it. To check this out, spend a few hours—or a weekend—getting everything in place. Chances are, you'll feel much better when you enter your office and see it well organized.

However, there is a big difference between *fixing* this problem and *resolving* it. You can take a weekend to clean up your office and you've *fixed* the situation. But, as you can imagine, in another week or two, your office will look just the same as it did prior to the fix, unless you put a *system* in place to keep your office uncluttered.

There are two systems that work. The best is to take the last ten minutes that you're in your office and to use that time to put everything in it's place. Next best is to take about a half hour to an hour every Friday to get your office back into shape. Why doesn't the second option work as well as the first? Because on a Friday afternoon, you're tempted to start your weekend early rather than do a clean-up!

SERVE QUALITY CLIENTS

Monitor your practice so that you accept only the highest quality clients. You can't—and shouldn't—work with everyone. Your quality of life is greatly reduced by clients who don't pay, who have unreasonable expectations and demands, who are unpleasant or uncooperative, or who are "high maintenance" in any way. If you currently have some of these undesirable clients, fire them (ethically, of course) or don't accept any more work from them. And if you're not sure who the undesirable clients are who need to be let go, just ask your staff. They are the ones typically who have to put up with the undesirable behavior even more than you do!

Even better, don't let these undesirable clients into your practice to begin with. Develop a screening system that looks for the "red flags" that identify potential problems—such as clients who have already been to other lawyers about their issues, who act entitled or rude on the phone, who call in a state of panic and demand instant service, who obviously are looking to get the cheapest price as their first objective, who are openly hostile and disparaging about the legal profession, and who have unrealistic or unreasonable expectations, etc. Each practice area will have some specific "red flags." For example, in a family law practice, a high level of spousal animosity might indicate an irrational client who could be very high maintenance and whom you probably want to turn down. In a personal injury practice, you might refer out a client whose matter is worth less than a specified amount.

BUILD A GREAT WORK TEAM

The quality of your law practice boils down to two main factors: the quality of your clients and the quality of your staff. This means that you need to take a hard look at the people on your team—be they legal assistants, receptionists, associates, even partners—and decide if they are, indeed, the "right" people. You don't want your practice to turn into a rehab center, limping along with people who do not have the skills they really need or who are destructive to the team in some way.

Of course, this means that you must hire people carefully if you want to minimize having to get rid of someone later on. Many lawyers, not really trained in hiring staff, resort to "intuitive hiring." They interview someone, get a good "vibe" about the person and, eager to have the position filled so they can get back to their practices, hire the person. Such hiring leads to a successful hire about fifteen percent of the time.

To raise the odds to about seventy-five percent (not perfect, but much better!), you'll need to put a hiring system in place. This would involve establishing careful criteria for the kind of person you want based upon the job description of the position you want to fill, careful interviewing, and, of course, being sure to check references. Skills testing (typing, grammar, filing, attention to detail, proofreading) and behavioral assessments (for example, DISC or Myers-Briggs) are extremely helpful. Hiring with a ninety-day probation period is critical, including a performance review at the end of the ninety-days.

You'll want to take your time hiring—hard as it may be. If you're not sure you've found the right person, keep looking.

In contrast, you'll want to fire quickly when you realize the person is not the employee you thought s/he would be. Set specific goals for a new hire for that first ninety days and, if problems become apparent, let that person go. Looking back on employees who "didn't work out" —or who are still in your firm and causing problems—typically you'll find that the warning signs were apparent in the first ninety days of their employment.

CONTROL INTERRUPTIONS

Studies of law offices have shown that an interruption takes an average of seven minutes, plus three minutes to recover. And that most attorneys have an average of ten interruptions per day. Add this time up and you'll quickly realize that you are losing over eight hours a week to interruptions! (You might want to multiply 400 hours—eight hours per week for fifty weeks a year, allowing two weeks for vacation—by your hourly rate so see how interruptions are affecting your pocketbook!).

Of course, some interruptions are necessary; they are part of doing business. But the idea is to control those interruptions that are not. So ask yourself, "Who—or what—is typically interrupting me during my day?"

If you are like most attorneys, it is likely that you allow your staff to interrupt you more than they need to. A way around this problem is to call a five-minute "huddle" when you first arrive at the office and, if needed, to schedule two or three other "huddles" during the day. Instead of your staff trying to corner you on the way to the restroom or lunch, they know that you will make yourself available during the scheduled "huddle" and they'll get their questions answered at that time. Most of their questions can wait a few hours; the ones that can't are legitimate interruptions.

Or maybe you have colleagues or staff who like to socialize. They plop down in a chair in your office and begin talking. You feel awkward or unfriendly telling them that they need to leave so you can get some work done. Closing your door is a first step in eliminating this problem. Tell people beforehand that you are going to close your door for specific periods of time when you're working on production, and ask them to respect your effort to improve your time management. You might even post a "Do Not Disturb" or "Production in Progress" sign on your door. Chances are others in your office will begin doing the same thing when they realize how much it helps them maintain control of their time.

Perhaps you interrupt yourself! You work on something for awhile and then find yourself calling a friend, looking up a sale on the internet, reading a blog, picking up a new file in the middle of working on another one, etc. Being aware of these internal distractions—and resigning yourself to carving out specific time periods for total concentration on your production work—can help tremendously. If you are highly distractible—or even have Attention Deficit Disorder— try listening to chamber music on headphones when you want to concentrate (reading, writing briefs, looking through documents, etc.). The repetitive nature of chamber music and the fact the music is without words make this a very helpful technique for improving both concentration and retention. Note: You will not get the same effect just by having this music in the room; it needs to be coming "right into your ears" via a headset.

CALENDAR YOUR PRODUCTION TIME

Whether it's writing briefs, doing research, analyzing a file, planning a deposition, or any of a number of technical lawyer tasks, you need to carve out "production time" when you can concentrate fully and without interruption. This can be a "power hour" every day or several hours, perhaps divided between morning and afternoon. The idea is to create a time template in which you block out the necessary production time each day, giving a copy of the template to everyone on your team so they know when you are not to be interrupted and allowing them to run interference for you when someone calls or appears unexpectedly (with the exception of a short list of people you may have asked to be put through to you). In court often? You can block out "court time" on your calendar for, say, mornings—but use that time for production if you don't have to go.

Using a time template can take some getting used to—and usually requires several weeks of experimentation before you get it "right" for you—but it is a powerful productivity tool that will greatly reduce the stress of a busy law practice.

SCHEDULE REPETITIVE PERSONAL TASKS

Rather than waiting to "have a few moments" or have a "break in schedule" to accomplish some personal task, write these into your daily schedule just as if they were client appointments or meetings. Perhaps it is a haircut every six weeks, a manicure bi-weekly, lunch with your child at school once a month, exercise, etc. Go ahead and write these into your schedule. Can they be changed? Of course. But the understanding is that if one of these needs to be cancelled on a particular day, *it is rescheduled* rather than disappearing from your calendar with an "Oh well. I'll try to make it the next time."

LEARN THE POWER OF "NO"

Whether it is with your clients, friends, relatives, family members, colleagues, vendors, or just about anybody, there are times you need to firmly say "no." You can't do everything and you can't please everybody; you have to pick and choose your activities according to your priorities. I like to call this concept "delicious self-care."

You see, we're all like bags of chocolate chip cookies. When your bag is full, you have plenty of cookies spilling out the top to give to your family, your community, your work, etc. But if you're down to just a few crumbs in the bottom of your bag, you're stressed out, probably grumpy, and can be setting yourself up for stress-related illnesses. That's why you need—and deserve—to keep your bag full! And it is impossible to keep your bag full if you say "yes" to everything asked of you.

Remember, "No" is a complete sentence!

SAY "NO" BY SAYING "YES"

In those situations when you think you can't really say "no", there is another way. The magic words are, "Let me tell you what I can do." The idea is that when someone asks something of you, you agree to do a small part that you're willing to do, but not the whole thing.

For example, let's say your child's teacher calls at 7 p.m. and says, "You know, we're having a bake sale at the school tomorrow and we're running short. You make those wonderful Italian cream cakes, and I was wondering if you could please make one tonight and bring it to the school tomorrow for the sale?"

Not wanting to say a flat-out "no," instead you say something like, "Well, let me tell you what I can do. I have some frozen lemon bars in the fridge and I'll be happy to send them tomorrow." For a work example, let's say an associate stops by at 5 p.m., just before you're ready to leave the office, and says,

"I need a summary of the such-and-such-file. Can you have it for me by noon tomorrow?" Knowing that your morning is booked—and not wanting to sit up half the night preparing this document—you say, "Let me tell you what I can do. I can give you an outline of the important points in that file by 11 a.m."

In other words, you agree to do something that requires much less of your time than what the person actually is requesting. In this way, you are being very cooperative, yet clearly protecting your time. It's not foolproof, but works much more often than not.

UTILIZE "THE FOUR D'S"

When we think about an upcoming task—whether it's cleaning out a stack of magazines, setting up an orientation program for new hires, considering planning a firm marketing event, or any of an unlimited variety of projects that cross our minds—we often resort to some version of "I'll think about it later." This delay tactic just creates more "to do's" that wander around in the backs of our minds, sapping our energy and making us feel overwhelmed. "The Four D's" Tool was created to solve this problem and is an outstanding time management tool. Here's how it works, using the stack of magazines example.

The first "D" stands for "Decide it!" In other words, at the time when your eye lands on that stack of magazines and you think, "Something must be done about it"—you make an immediate decision about it (that first "D"). And your decision will be one of the other three "D's": Do It, Delegate It, or Dump It. In other words, you'll decide once and for all how you are going to deal with those magazines.

If you decide on "Do It," schedule the time you'll do it on your calendar, even if it is three weekends or three months away. By placing it on your schedule, you no longer have to worry about it because you know that it is in your calendar and won't be forgotten.

If you decide on "Delegate It," give the task to someone else, making clear exactly how you want that pile of magazines to be handled and when you'd like for the job to be completed. For example, you might ask the person to go through the stack and cut out all articles on a particular issue, putting them into a folder for you to read later.

The third option is, simply, to "Dump It." If you haven't looked at that stack in six months, how likely is it that you really need to read it? In the case of stacks of magazines (or trade journals), this is often the most realistic and preferable option. Then create a system for how you want to deal with those publications in the future: cancel the subscription, take five minutes when you get the publication to look through the Table of Contents and cut out any articles you're really interested in, ask your assistant to catalogue specific topics for you, etc.

The key, of course, is that first "D." That's where you basically handle the issue, making an immediate decision to utilize one of the other three "D's."

This is also a great approach when you go through your inbox. You decide what to do with each piece of paper, file or item as you get to it rather than postponing your decision to a later time.

BATCH SIMILAR TASKS

One easy way to increase your productivity is to batch similar tasks together in scheduled time periods. Instead of letting a voice mail, phone call, or email distract you, set aside two or three half-hour time periods when you will perform these activities. Make sure your assistant knows these times so she can relay the information to clients when they call. There will be exceptions, of course, but they need to be exceptions rather than the rule. This one step will greatly increase your ability to concentrate on your work.

Of course, those calls that you'll need to return should be "quickie" calls; otherwise, you may find yourself getting tied up for an hour and a half or more when you call people back. This problem can be solved by having your assistant find out, whenever possible, why the person is calling. If she can determine that the call will need more than five minutes, she can schedule the caller for an in-person or phone visit (blocked out on your calendar template during set times for fifteen or thirty minutes). When you return a call, if you realize that the caller needs more time, let the person know that you can't do the matter justice in just a few minutes, and schedule them for a phone or in-person appointment. This way you'll keep your half-hour call-back times on schedule.

DO A WEEKLY PLANNING SESSION

Once a week, typically on Friday afternoons or Monday mornings, sit down with your calendar in front of you and plan out your week. Sounds like a no-brainer, but many people don't take the time to do it.

During your planning session, be sure to look four to six weeks ahead in your calendar. This way you'll be able to anticipate in advance how much time you need to block out for specific tasks in the week you're currently working on. This procedure ensures that you won't come up short on a deadline or wind up pulling all-nighters in an effort to meet your commitments.

Having a weekly planning time with your staff is also helpful. It gives everyone an opportunity to know what others are working on, what the priorities are for that week, and to rearrange their individual schedules to accommodate the work that must be done.

PLAN A VACATION

Let's face it, getting totally away from the office for periods of time is sanity protection (if you respond to email and phone calls, that's cheating!). The problem is, scheduling vacation time often becomes one of those "when I get to it" items. What usually happens, of course, is that the vacation never comes—or gets delayed—because you look at your continually filling schedule and think "There's just no time!"

The secret is to plan months ahead. Decide when you want to go on vacation and block out that week or two *before* you get even close to scheduling that time on your calendar. Doing this allows you to plan your schedule around your vacation rather than the other way around.

And while you're at it, use the first day back from vacation as a "shadow day." That means that you are back from vacation that day—but technically, people are told you won't be back until the day *after*. This keeps the day you come back to the office free for you to catch up with your phone calls, email and voice mail, to get focused on what is coming up, to re-set your priorities for that week, and to re-orient yourself back into work without driving yourself crazy.

USE LUNCH FOR MARKETING

Marketing is really all about building relationships, and what better way to do that than to use your lunch time to meet with referral sources and influencers who can send you business. The problem is that marketing is often the first thing to go when your schedule gets tight. Using your lunch hours for this purpose not only helps your business, but the break in your day gives you a mental boost that you just don't get sitting at your desk munching on a sandwich.

DELEGATE WHENEVER POSSIBLE

Consider your hourly fee. Now ask yourself, "What tasks am I doing that could be done by someone who earns much less per hour?" The answer will give you an idea about what you need to start delegating. Making copies and sending faxes are not something you need a law degree to do.

If you realize that you need to delegate but don't have a clue where to begin, make a list of everything you do. Just keep a pen and paper handy and jot down the tasks you find yourself doing over a two- or three-day period. Once you have your list, highlight all the items that only you can do; for example, going to court. Any task that requires the skill of an attorney would be on this list. If you have associates, ask yourself if it would be a better use of your time to have your associate(s) do a particular task. Also, highlight any task that is done so seldom that it wouldn't be worth your time to train someone on your staff to do it. These highlighted tasks are the ones you will keep for sure.

Next, with the remaining items on the list, mark the ones that you dislike or find boring. Those become obvious tasks to delegate. And, of course, delegate those tasks that can obviously be done by a less skilled/educated staff person (like copying and faxing).

Make sure that you give a clear explanation of exactly what you expect from the person whom you are delegating to. And keep tabs on them as appropriate. For example, with a person who is experienced at the task and trustworthy about deadlines, you might give her a deadline and tell her to get back in touch with you if she runs into any problems. With someone who is new at what you're asking her to do—or is poor about meeting deadlines—ask her to check in with you daily or weekly. In this way you will delegate effectively and not have the problem of someone doing the work poorly and giving you the excuse to say, "I knew I should have done it myself!"

ARRANGE SUPPORT SYSTEMS

If you have children, you want to have as many back-up systems as possible for days when they are ill as well as for those times when something unexpected comes up and you absolutely have to be at the office or in court. Talk with your network about sitters. Learn about places and caretakers that accept children on an as-needed basis if a child isn't well enough to return to school or to his regular daycare. This can be a difficult chore, but it is made easier by your being willing to ask people for these resources.

If you work in a firm with several attorneys, you might find a dry cleaning business that is willing to come to your office weekly to pick up and deliver. The same is true for car-washing services that will come to your office. It's good for their businesses—and good for your sanity to have less errands to run.

Look for gyms, yoga classes, places that have ready-to-go meals, massage therapists—any services of interest—in a location that is either near your office, near your home, or on your commute. The less time you spend driving around, the better.

HIRE HELP

Unless you find housework fascinating, hire someone to help you with it. I've had many clients who could well afford to have this kind of help, but don't do it because they think, "If I *can* do it, then I *should* do it!" In other words, it doesn't bother them to have someone at a gas station change the oil in their cars because they don't know how to do it themselves. But scrubbing a toilet or retrieving dust bunnies from under the bed, those things they can do! Be nice to yourself and give yourself permission to allow someone to help you even though you are very capable of doing the work yourself.

I had a client who had a thriving law practice, a child, and a significant other. She did have a housekeeper, but complained that she had tons of errands that took up her valuable time. What she wanted to do with her evenings was to spend time with her daughter and/or her boyfriend and to have some time for herself. The problem was solved when she hired a woman to do her errands. She paid the woman $50 per week to come to her house every Wednesday afternoon, do her grocery shopping, put the groceries away, deliver and pick up dry cleaning, pick her daughter up from school and drive her to gymnastics, run any other errands, and then fix a couple of casseroles that could be served for dinner when needed. She felt that her quality of life changed dramatically for the better just from this one investment, and that it was the best $50 a week she'd ever spent!

READ YOUR EMAIL INBOX ONLY ONCE

Most people glance at their email inbox when they have a spare moment and quickly read through the subject line or first part of the email. They might answer one or two of them and delete a few. But they leave many behind, thinking "I'll get to that one later" or "I need to think about that one before I respond." A few hours later, they go back to that inbox and have to read through those emails that were left behind all over again in order to decide what to do with them! This process can waste a tremendous amount of time.

Instead, set up some categories for your email. For example, you might have a category for each of the people in your office (or groups of people), a category for any organizations you belong to, a category called "To Read", even a category marked "Jokes." When you look at an email in your inbox and it can't be responded to and/or deleted within two minutes, send that email to the proper category to be reviewed later.

A real timesaver is to have a category marked "Waiting For." Let's say you send an email to someone requesting something from them. You blind copy yourself on any requests to others, and when the email copy that you originated comes back, you send it right to your "Wait For" file. At the end of the day, click on your "Wait For" file to remind yourself about what you're waiting for. You can quickly scan the list to see if there is anything urgent that you've expected, but not received, then re-email the person (or call them if it's really urgent!) to remind them about what you're missing. Many of the items won't be urgent because there is no critical deadline to meet or because you're willing to give the person more time to respond. With this system, you can leave work at the end of the day feeling secure that nothing has slipped your mind that you were supposed to receive and take care of immediately.

DO SOMETHING THAT INTERESTS YOU–BESIDES WORK!

All work and no play makes for a very dull life. It's important to take time for yourself to do those things that you enjoy doing. Whether it is playing a sport, reading novels, gardening, entertaining friends, learning to make a new gourmet dish, watching *Oprah* or *Cold Case Files* on Tivo, rollerblading, anything that is pleasurable for you, you need to take the time to do it.

It's helpful to think of things you enjoy that take varying amounts of time. An activity that requires most of a day, you might schedule once a month—like a photography outing. Then there are those things that take an hour or two—like meeting a friend for dinner or going to a movie. Each week, if possible, plan an activity you enjoy that takes an hour or two.

But don't forget all those activities that can be done in a half hour or less. A bubble bath, reading, a phone chat with your best friend, playing with your dog, watering plants, meditating—there are so many activities that you can squeeze into even the busiest of days.

THINK IN TERMS OF "INTEGRATION" RATHER THAN "BALANCE"

Actually, the concept of "life balance" is misleading. Balance implies equal time on each of the important aspects of your life, which would be a ridiculous goal! For example, let's say that spirituality is an important dimension in your life. It doesn't mean that you would necessarily want to spend hours in a spiritual practice. For you, going to church once a week, joining a Bible study class, meditating on a daily basis, taking a course on the great religions of the world, readily a daily spiritual affirmation, planning a nature walk monthly—any one of these might fulfill your spiritual needs.

Rather than "life balance," I prefer the term "life integration." This concept allows for each of the important areas of your life to be fulfilled without trying to "balance" everything out.

A FINAL CAUTION

Hopefully, you've found that at least some of the above "tips" would be helpful. You feel encouraged and hopeful that your life can be less hectic and more fulfilling. And it can be. But beware of the temptation to plunge in and tackle too many tips at once, which will only lead to overwhelm and frustration. Instead, pick one or two items to implement at any one time, adding others after you integrate those. People who are working with a Practice Management Coach often take at least a year to integrate them successfully.

Remember, when you work to put these tips in place, you're just adding cookies to your bag!

APPENDIX

MORE THOUGHTS FROM THE INTERVIEWEES

So readers could get a little deeper insight into the views of the women attorneys who provided the information for this book, the interviewees were invited to contribute a brief essay on whatever topic they wanted related to their practices or their law careers. Four of them chose to write.

Two essays are about "lessons learned" from clients. One describes the author's practice philosophy. And one describes overcoming discrimination and finding one's personal power.

Enjoy.

WE'RE NOT SO BAD AFTER ALL!

Shannon McLin Carlyle and Mario Villella

It was a typically crazy evening in the life of a working mom. I picked up our three kids from school and rushed back to the office to sign some motions before the FedEx truck arrived. Our oldest son, Blair, was playing "Winthrop" in *The Music Man*, so we were scurrying to get everyone home, eat dinner, and do homework. Those tasks done, I rushed off with Blair to play rehearsal, while my husband stayed home with the other kids.

At the theatre, I sat in a chair and watched the director work with the actors. I enjoyed the chance to relax and recover from the day, finally free of phone calls and e-mails. During a break, the performers gathered in the lobby to get a drink and talk. There, a dark-haired young man in his mid-twenties approached me and introduced himself. His name was Mario Villella, and he played the part of Marcellus in the play. He complimented my son on the work he was doing and we chatted.

I learned that Mario had just gotten his degree in Arts and Performance at the University of Texas at Dallas, and had moved back to Florida to become a youth minister. He and his wife, Heidi, were new to the area and he had read about the auditions in the paper and just came down. After telling me a little about his background, Mario asked, "So, what do *you* do?" I responded with a nervous laugh, "Well, I'm a lawyer . . . but please don't hold that against me." When he acted surprised at my reaction, I explained that I never knew how people were going to react after I tell them my profession. I'm sure we've all experienced the off-hand joke after we tell a stranger about our profession. The conversation was cut short when the director called the cast back to the stage.

A few days later, we were back at play practice and I saw Mario again. During a break, he strolled over to say hi and to tell me how my apologetic comment about my profession made him think of the bad rap lawyers face. I thanked him, and knew that I had made a lasting friend. "I wrote this when I got home the other night," he said, while handing me the neatly folded papers that he had pulled from his back pocket. "It just bothered me that you didn't seem proud of what you do." On the paper was written the following:

WHY I LIKE LAWYERS

By Mario Villella

There is a truth that most people I know acknowledge as being universal: "Human beings do bad things." Now, there is much debate as to *why* this is true. Some people believe we learn bad behavior from our environment. Other people think bad behaviors stem from our genetic code and the general health of our minds and bodies. Other people think the problem is a spiritual problem in our natures that all people have when they are born. Whatever the cause, most everyone agrees that people do bad things that damage other people and their property.

For this reason, we here in America (and every other nation and people group for that matter) have laws. Civil and Criminal laws are set up to:

- Restrain and/or deter people from doing the bad things they have a proclivity to do.
- Punish people who choose to hurt others.
- Compensate people who are the victims of abuse or negligence of others.

And every single person who works in the field of law plays an important part in doing those three things. Police officers, judges, legislators, jurors, military personnel, politicians, and investigators are just a few of the many people who commit a large portion of their life to this process of restraining evil, punishing law breakers, and protecting innocent victims.

And for the most part, the people who hold these positions are respected for the important work they do. There is one group of people, however, that play an equally important role in this system, and yet for some reason they are not given the same respect. The group to which I'm referring is: Lawyers. Lawyers are repeatedly joked about, often held in derision, and sometimes openly hated. This is tragic. If it weren't for lawyers:

- Innocent people who are unable to defend themselves in court would be convicted of crimes they didn't commit.
- Guilty people who are especially talented in deception would not be punished for their crimes.

- Companies would be able to advertise falsely with no consequence.
- Food and drug producers could easily distribute harmful products to the public.
- Divorces would be an even more difficult process where the spouse with the least amount of intelligence and/or communication skills would simply lose out on their fair share of the assets.
- Artists would have their creative works stolen and/or reproduced without permission, and they would be unable to seek out any sort of just compensation.
- The constitutions of the federal and state governments would lose their significance.
- Their power would slowly erode away.
- Crime would escalate, as people realized no one was professionally or occupationally committed to prosecute crimes with quality and excellence.
- Legal errors would never be overturned through the appeals process.
- Victims of negligence would rarely see restitution.
- Governments would be able to abuse their powers over the citizens in their jurisdictions.

I really could go on and on. But to sum it all up, lawyers help restrain evil, punish lawbreakers, and protect innocent citizens. Sure, there are corrupt lawyers who abuse their role and actually help further evil, protect lawbreakers, and punish innocent citizens. But that is true of all of the "law" professions; there are corrupt judges, police officers, legislators, and politicians. Frankly, there are corrupt people in every field, even those outside the legal profession, including doctors, firefighters, teachers, priests, janitors, and journalists. The reason this is true goes back to the first point: Human beings do bad things.

The fact that some lawyers are "corrupt" is not evidence that we "don't need lawyers." It is actually evidence supporting the other side. We do need them. As long as there are corrupt people in any field in this country, we need lawyers to help us to restrain and punish them while protecting the victims they hurt.

Mario's words touched me, and made me think about the comment that motivated his writing. I am proud of my profession, and of the work we do. I realized that comments like mine play into a societal stereotype that our profession is somewhat less than honorable, and that perhaps we as lawyers are not proud of our profession. Thanks to Mario's inspiration, I vowed to answer the question in the future by proudly saying that I am a lawyer, and to leave it at that.

***Shannon McLin Carlyle** formed The Carlyle Appellate Law Firm in 1997 after serving as a law clerk at the Fifth District Court of Appeal. The Carlyle Appellate Law Firm has offices in Orlando and The Villages and is a member of The Florida Appellate Alliance, PLC, a statewide alliance of three appellate firms with offices in North, Central, and South Florida. Ms. Carlyle is Board Certified by The Florida Bar in Appellate Practice, is a certified circuit court and appellate mediator, and is AV rated by Martindale-Hubbell. She serves on the Executive Council of The Florida Bar's Appellate Practice Section, and was recently elected to the Board of Directors of the Florida Justice Association's Women's Caucus. She has served on the faculty of the Family Law and Appellate Practice Sections' CLE programs, lecturing on the appellate aspects relating to family law and litigation in general. Ms. Carlyle was recognized in 2006 and 2007 by Law & Politics as a Florida Superlawyer in appellate practice, and is a member of Florida Trend's 2006 Florida Legal Elite in appellate practice.*

LESSONS FROM A CLIENT

By Nora Riva Bergman

During my years as an employment law attorney, I met many people who had been treated badly by their employers. Some had been fired unfairly; harassed; or simply ignored. When I heard their stories, I would often have to tell them that, although they had been treated badly, there was nothing illegal in the way they were treated. I could only help them if their employer had broken a law. This was difficult for many to hear. Some refused to listen. Some blamed me for not understanding or caring. Others refused to accept any responsibility for anything that happened to them.

Then there was Mechy. Mechy came to this country as a young girl from Cuba. She started high school and taught herself English. She graduated, and began a career in modeling before becoming the first woman hired as a firefighter for the City of Tampa in the seventies. During her twenty years with the fire department, she raised two sons (one of whom is now an attorney), cared for her parents, and built a wonderful life with her firefighter husband, Jesse. She also spoke out about discrimination in the workplace, and she lived through—and worked through—years of discrimination on the job. Notice, I didn't say Mechy was a victim of discrimination. She is not a victim of anything.

I had the privilege of representing Mechy during her last years with the department. Throughout the litigation of the case, Mechy made no excuses for anything. She kept working. Although she was passed over for several promotions during this time, she kept working. She kept doing the right thing until her case eventually settled. Then she went back to school and earned a Master's Degree. She is now pursuing a successful second career.

As law students, we're taught there is no such thing as a perfect client, and certainly that's true. Nobody's perfect. But Mechy taught me a lot about integrity during the time we worked together. Regardless of the personal consequences, she always chose to do the right thing. She spoke out about discrimination, even when she knew her actions would affect her own career. She walked the talk.

I'm proud to say that Mechy remains a friend to this day.

As a business coach for attorneys, ***Nora Rive Bergman*** *is dedicated to helping them create the lives and law practices they dreamed of when they were in law school. She knows the frustrations that attorneys experience everyday and is committed to helping them change their lives for the better. She has practiced as an employment law attorney and certified mediator, and has served as a professor at both Stetson University College of Law and the University of South Florida, teaching courses in alternative dispute resolution and negotiation. In addition, Nora has been a speaker at conferences for the American Bar Association and The Florida Bar. She has also served as the Executive Director of the St. Petersburg Bar Association.*

Nora is a graduate of the prestigious Leadership Development Program at Eckerd College and is certified in the Conflict Dynamics Profile developed by Eckerd to help individuals and organizations learn how to deal with conflict constructively. She received an undergraduate degree in journalism, summa cum laude, from the University of South Florida and her J.D., cum laude, from Stetson University College of Law, where she was a member of the law review and served as a mentor for incoming students.

OBSERVATIONS AND PERSPECTIVES

By Latonia Early-Hubelbank

From the beginning I found matrimonial law to be a great challenge—the challenge is to see if you can have a reasonably happy client who is optimistic about the future when the divorce process is completed. And that, of course, is not easy in our legal field.

The truth is that, in most divorce cases, the primary fight is about money. It's hard to argue with the numbers in a divorce case—but it's easy to argue with the other side over how to allocate them. That's why it's important to know who the opposing attorney is—and get everyone to sit down together. As long as the other side isn't willfully trying to derail the process, we can usually work through it. But attorneys can sometimes be an impediment to a resolution. So one of the first things I do is find out who the other spouse's attorney is. Just by doing that, I can often tell how long the case is going to take and how difficult the resolution is going to be.

The level of emotion in any divorce has a way of impacting the quality of decisions people make—part of our job, as attorneys, is to ensure that decisions are made for sound reasons, based on facts and real needs, rather than on the emotion of the moment. Clients will tell me, "Oh, I'm fine, I've got a good support network." Yet an intense level of emotion may still be there.

My client is the driver to a case—and I am their advisor and foot soldier. Every case is a partnership, and I make sure that we work well and closely together.

As a young lawyer, I've faced some challenges. Assumptions are always going to be made about you when you are young. An older judge or an old-school attorney is going to test you. Of the major players in Nassau county, many of them know me by now. But some of the older attorneys will still try to push me around.

I'm not a confrontational person. I'm conciliatory, and always try to be reasonable. But at the same time I always defend my client's interests very firmly. I think most of the legal community knows that. I won't be intimidated. I'm known for being tough when I have to be.

I think part of my success is that I make good resources available to all my clients. I refer them to the right counseling professionals if they need it, and I educate them about the law and the likeliest scenarios of their cases.

All of my clients get through the process—and through all of it, they are building hope for their futures.

YOU'VE COME A LONG WAY, BABY—REALLY!

By Karen L. Marvel

I was raised in the seventies, when women's equality and the Equal Rights Amendment were hot topics in my politically conscious home. My mother worked full time by choice in public relations, and I learned from her that professional females do succeed in a male dominated world. As a child, I broke through gender barriers with impunity. Bobbie Lynn Earl and I were the first girls in fifth grade allowed to raise and lower the flags in front of school. I was the first girl tuba player in middle school, high school, and at my college. My law school class at Texas Tech was about forty percent female, so I naively assumed that other women had made the inroads into the legal profession for me and that I would sail right into a legal career as a "lawyer"—not as a "female lawyer."

My first job out of law school was with a firm where I had clerked the two previous summers. The senior partner, Oliver Heard, was a brash, overbearing, brilliant man and a very skilled trial attorney. Many lawyers underestimated his trial and negotiation skills—in part because of his girth and in part because he had developed a multi-million dollar statewide practice handling delinquent tax collection for cities and counties. Oliver was hired to try and "pull the ox out of the ditch" in a complicated probate case. A post trial conference was set up with all the attorneys at one of the highest brow of the locally-based law firms. Although I had just started at the firm and had done very little work on the case, Oliver took me along to the conference.

Before this meeting, I had very little exposure to corporate law firms. I worked in the family law area of our practice and saw mostly solo practitioners. Their conference room was quite opulent, complete with a uniformed maid in the corner bringing everyone coffee. I took a seat at the conference table next to Oliver—an older associate from our firm sat on his other side. Everyone at the table was male and older. I realized after sitting down that there were chairs lined up all around the walls of the conference room, and all those chairs were also filled with male lawyers who looked a little closer to my age.

I pulled out my legal pad and prepared to take notes as the meeting started. Finally, someone asked Oliver, "Why is she here?" Oliver mumbled (as he did when the subject matter was inconsequential) that I worked for him, failing to mention my name or introduce me to anyone at the table.

The meeting proceeded. Oliver commanded the room (as usual) and a couple of issues were resolved. When we adjourned, I was treated as furniture by all the other attorneys as they shook hands and made small talk with Oliver and one another. Later, when I asked the older associate about what happened, he said they all probably thought I was Oliver's secretary!

Oliver did not mean to be rude or demeaning; everybody already knew the other associate and it did not occur to him to include me as part of the team. After that day, I learned not to be shy or timid, and to just introduce myself in the future. By the way, Oliver resolved the case quite favorably for our clients.

Later that year, I represented an attorney in a nasty divorce and custody battle. I had a hearing about the scope of pretrial discovery before a retired visiting judge. When I got back to the office, I called my client and told him I wasn't going to bill him for the hearing because the judge had totally ignored me—so much so that I may as well have not shown up at all. I mentioned my loss to Oliver in passing. He told me to file a motion for rehearing and that he would come along.

At the next hearing when Oliver and I approached the bench, the judge heard the identical argument I had made at the previous hearing—but this time, he ruled in our favor. I was not only the only female lawyer this judge treated poorly—unless the lawyer was especially attractive or had a beautiful client. Luckily in our state we can object to a visiting judge on each case, and I never appeared in front of that judge again (even to get an agreed reset order signed).

Fast forward eleven years. I was appointed to represent a mentally ill man with chronic catatonic schizophrenia on a hearing for involuntary commitment to the State Hospital. I demanded a jury trial. During the State's case, I looked around the courtroom and realized that all the participants in the trial—me, the judge, the prosecutors, even the bailiff and court reporter—were female. No problems with people not being introduced in that courtroom! When I commented on it to the judge after the trail, she smiled and said, "Well, it's about time!"

As I write this, I rapidly approach the twentieth anniversary of passing my bar exam. I no longer feel like furniture in a meeting and I refuse to be ignored by any judge in a hearing. I regularly practice before judges who were licensed after me. For the most part, I like my practice and my choices.

Unfortunately, I still see many female lawyers who have the same experience as their male counterparts but are making less money. A woman who scales back on her hours to be available for her children still hurts her chance to be a partner—but a man who does it gets a "Father of the Year" trophy. I chose a more sane (for me) path of law practice that does not require 2,300 billable hours a year and reviewing documents at 4:30 a.m. For those people who can do the partnership grind, I say "bravo." For everybody else, I remind you to look at your life goals and plan the goals of your career around them. I did the "Mommy track" for several years and my salary reflected it—but I chose my children over career advancement. Now that I'm a wife and mother, I prefer to be home instead of sitting at the office. That means I come home for dinner and then get on the computer after I kiss my kids goodnight. I write and lecture in continuing education because I love it, so I integrated the time it takes into my practice and use it as part of my marketing. Find your balance.

Those career counselors were right when they said to do what you like and the money will follow. Figure out what area of practice you enjoy and then you can make a good living. You do no one—you, your clients, or the courts—any favors when you only show up at work for the paycheck and benefits.

***Karen L. Marvel** is a partner at Sinkin & Marvel in San Antonio, Texas, where she practices child support enforcement, handling cases throughout Texas involving unusual situations or large child support arrearages. She graduated from McMurry University in Abilene, Texas (B.A., 1984), and Texas Tech University School of Law (J.D., 1987). Karen is a frequent writer, lecturer, and course director for continuing legal education courses in Texas. She is active in local bar activities and has held numerous offices in the Family Law Section of the San Antonio Bar Association. Karen is married to an attorney and they have three children. She serves on the Board of the Autism Society of Greater San Antonio, teaches Sunday School and is a board member of the PTA. Before she had a husband and children, she had outside hobbies; she now finds that running after her children, juggling schedules, and reading minds (or trying to) keeps her very busy.*

THE ATTICUS PRACTICE DIAGNOSTIC

For an objective evaluation of your law practice, consider the Atticus Practice Diagnostic. This 120-question evaluation assesses four critical factors necessary for success: Time Management and Productivity, Client Development, Staffing Issues, and Cash Flow/Profitability. The questions are emailed or faxed to you and take about twenty minutes to complete. Dr. Craig will schedule a one-hour debrief session by telephone and will give you specific recommendations to implement. The diagnostic is $175 with a money-back satisfaction guarantee.

To schedule, please email judi@atticusonline.com or call 210.824.2776.